Contents

training using
DRAMA

training using
DRAMA

successful development techniques
from theatre & improvisation

KAT KOPPETT

KOGAN
PAGE

First published in the United States in 2001, as *Training to Imagine,* by Stylus Publishing LLC, 22883 Quicksilver Drive, Sterling, Virginia 20166

First published in Great Britain in 2002 by Kogan Page Limited

Kogan Page Limited
120 Pentonville Road
London N1 9JN

© Kat Koppett, 2002

British Library Cataloguing in Publication Data

A CIP record for this book is available from the British Library.

ISBN 0 7494 3704 9

Typeset by Saxon Graphics Ltd, Derby
Printed and bound in Great Britain by Clays Ltd, St Ives plc

*To my parents for their patient endurance of my
improvisational path.
And to the unsung heroes of improv everywhere.*

Acknowledgements

It is difficult even to identify all of the people who have provided me with the knowledge, support and inspiration behind this book. In addition to each of the teachers, students and colleagues from whom I have learnt so much, I owe special debts to the following people:

- From the improv community:
  - *Freestyle Repertory Theatre*, especially Laura Livingston and Kenn Adams for their extraordinary artistic minds; and Michael Durkin, Sam Cohen, Michael Rock, Debbie Rabbai and Adam Felber for the years of fellowship and inspiration;
  - *Bay Area Theatresports*, especially Rebecca Stockley for opening doors and arms to me, and for her help as an improv historian; Carol Hazenfield, Tony Lijphart, Rich Ross, Gary Barth and Dan Klein for being my first West Coast teachers; Paul Killam, Rafe Chase and Kirk Livingston for their artistic leadership; Susan Snyder for her support in developing the corporate training wing, and her insight and encouragement as a writer; Stephen Kearin, Diane Rachel, Barbara Scott and Kirk Livingston for allowing me to quote them; and all the BATS companies and their members for so much joy and learning;
  - *Chicago City Limits*, for initiating my life as an improviser, especially my teachers, Chris Oyen, Terry Sommer, David Regal and Linda Gelman;
  - and the talented souls of *Unexpected Company*.
- From the business community:
  - *Alain Rostain of Creative Advantage*, who was a pioneer in recognizing the value of improv in the business setting;
  - *William Hall and Richard Dupell of Fratelli Bologna*, who continue to innovate, enlighten and entertain all sorts of communities using

improvisational theatre techniques, and who have mentored me in my quest to do the same;

– *Andy Kimball of QBInternational*, who, when he isn't providing me with fabulous professional opportunities, nurtures and accommodates me in my own endeavours to a dumbfounding degree;

– *Philip Mudd and John von Knorring*, my publishers, who said 'Yes' to the idea;

– *Helen Moss*, who edited the manuscript with just the right combination of eagle-eyed attention to detail and generous non-interference;

– and *Thiagi*, our guru, whether he likes it or not.

- Finally, from the rest of my life:
  – *my parents* for their writers' genes and their professional counsel;
  – *my brother* for his quiet wisdom and his ability to outjoke my improv buddies;
  – *my friends* Amy, Cameron, Darlene, Jo and Kimberly, for keeping the artistic torches burning;
  – and *Matt Richter*, my adviser, research assistant, first line editor and partner – for being my door Matt, my welcome Matt and, as of this edition, my husband too.

Introduction

I have been...part of various theatre companies, any one of which in its healthy state more nearly resembles a perfect community than any other group that I have encountered.

David Mamet, playwright, *True and False*

I remember vividly the moment I knew theatre techniques had value in business. In the late 1980s my standing as an unemployed actor prompted me to do two things: get a day job and start studying improvisational theatre. The job entailed teaching English as a second language (ESL) to Russian immigrants. It paid the rent. The improv classes provided fun, companionship and a sense that I was developing skills that I could transfer to my scripted work. Neither activity was meant to lead anywhere long term. But life is like improv. You do not know where you are going, just where you have been.

My job led to a position as a trainer and supervisor at the ESL school, which led to taking management-skills training with a consultant named Cal Sutliff. (The entire management staff was made up of actors, and we certainly needed supervisory training.) Cal took me under his wing, and eventually I was co-delivering people-skills courses with him at Cornell's School of Industrial and Labor Relations.

Meanwhile, I had joined Freestyle Repertory Theatre, an improvisational theatre company performing in the heart of Manhattan. In addition to performing completely improvised shows (no script, no pre-planning), Freestyle Rep taught improv classes. Soon after I joined the group, we began to offer team-building and creativity workshops for corporations. Because of my experience with training, embryonic though it was, I was charged with designing and delivering these programmes.

Although the sessions went well, I grew uneasy. Were the skills of improv and theatre really useful in corporate settings, or were we selling snake oil?

Were the actor's abilities to captivate an audience and play different roles transferable? Was the improviser's need to accept ideas, create collaboratively, exercise spontaneity and take risks actually of use to professional business people? I decided I should find out, so I enrolled in a Master's course in organizational psychology at Columbia University.

My coursework at Columbia provided valuable theories and practices that have enhanced my consulting and training. Luckily, studies supported the work we had been doing, and supplied the professional vocabulary and context for our work. What most dispelled my doubt about the value of theatrical training, though, was a single incident that occurred within the first two months of the course.

In a human resources survey course, we were assigned topics for group presentations. Most of the presentations were standard reports – students standing before the class holding note cards, nervously making sure that they had every detail correct. My group had been charged with discussing performance reviews, and we put together a series of sketches, illustrating first the wrong way and then the right way to run them. The sketches were very simple. I am sure we did not work any harder than anyone else or possess any special talent. But the other students and tutor loved us. Seeing us having fun, interacting with the audience and injecting humour into the topic impressed them. Students commented to me on the presentation for the rest of my time on the course. They always said they had enjoyed it and – this is the exciting part – many of them added that they still remembered the four points we had discussed.

As I continued to develop the communication and creativity-skills courses that I was offering, my belief that improv, especially, has something to offer business was reinforced. Every now and then, I am influenced by the scepticism I encounter when discussing my work. 'Oh, that's just fluff,' a relative says. Or a potential client challenges, 'Yes, soft skills are all well and good – what about the bottom line?' I never stay unsure for long, though. People *want* the kinds of interactions that performers – especially improvisers – take for granted. We get to express ourselves creatively, play together, have our ideas honoured and our failures not only forgiven but celebrated. It is impossible to miss the transformational effects of the work, even for the sceptics. The links to the bottom line have become clearer and clearer. Innovation soars. Teams resolve conflicts and work more productively. My workshop participants retain more of the information I disseminate, and the managers I coach report increased levels of comfort and effectiveness.

Bolstered by the success of the work, I started a business, StoryNet LLC, which uses storytelling and theatre techniques in training and consulting. I took on a position as the corporate division director at Bay

Area Theatresports in San Francisco, delivering improv training to business people. I infused the more traditional sales coaching and presentation-skills training that I deliver with exercises drawn from drama and improv schools. Increasingly, I found myself presenting at training conferences and holding train-the-trainer sessions, passing along the wisdom and techniques of the theatre to other professionals. The intention of *Training Using Drama* is to present drama and improvisation techniques in a way that allows trainers and managers to adapt the techniques to their own environments. You need not have a background in theatre or a desire to perform to use these tools. All you need is a wish to enhance learning and infuse your environment with creativity, teamwork and effective communication.

Having spoken about improvisation and drama in the same breath till this point, I should mention that, although the skills of improvisation and traditional theatre overlap a great deal, the two communities have tended to maintain very separate identities. Traditional actors often have had more formal training in voice, speech, movement and text analysis. Improvisers, of course, tend to be more comfortable making things up on the spot, and, in addition, have been more formally schooled in collaborative and narrative techniques. *Training Using Drama* focuses to a great degree on the language and techniques of improvisational theatre. Here's why. In improvisation, performers work as actors, playwrights and directors simultaneously. This state mirrors life in a more literal way than does the more traditional theatre situation in which the roles are neatly divided. With the exception of formal presentations, working life comes without the benefit of scripts and rehearsals. In addition, the vocabulary and activities that improvisers have developed for creating collaboratively are especially useful in business settings as organizations flatten and change accelerates. Of course, many of these techniques are used in traditional theatre settings as well.

Specifically, this text will provide:

- explanations of the major improvisational theatre concepts and techniques, as well as applicable traditional theatre skills;
- links to training and management skills;
- a series of exercises suitable for use in professional training environments.

I have not set out to write a comprehensive manual for performers, a complete list of theatre games or a complete guide to effective training. Rather, I have included here those concepts and exercises from the theatre world that I have found offer the most to trainers and managers.

The most daunting task I faced in writing this book was tracking the origins of the exercises. The development of improvisational theatre, especially, has itself been improvisational. Someone has an idea or creates a format and, before you know it, there are companies around the world adapting and building on the inspiration. Therefore, it is difficult to attribute inventions. Intellectual property has become a hot issue with the advent of the Internet. Improvisers have been struggling with it for years. I have been present for the creation of some wonderful exercises, which only weeks later I saw attributed elsewhere. I made peace with the impossibility of tracking the origin of each activity when Rebecca Stockley, a Bay Area TheatreSports' founder, dean of their school and a thought leader in the West Coast improv community, told me this story.

When she was writing her book *Improvisation through TheatreSports* (1989), Stockley found herself searching for the creators of games, too. Her quest for the origins of one specific game, 'Sound ball' (called 'Invisible balls' on page 32), sent her from person to person for months. She went to the improviser she had learnt it from. That person sent her to someone else and so forth. Eventually, she was referred to Roberta Maguire, the woman who had brought the Theatresports format from Canada to the western United States. A few days after she received the referral, Rebecca ran into Roberta on a ferry.

'Roberta!' she said. 'Just the woman I've been meaning to call. Where did you learn "Sound ball"?'

Roberta paused for a moment, thought and said, 'Gee, Rebecca, I think I learned it from you!'

Although Rebecca continued to be as vigilant as possible in her attributions, she realized the Herculean nature of her task. I have attempted the same vigilance, and I recount Rebecca's story not as an excuse for any omissions or mistakes but as apology and explanation. If there is a reader who has better information, I would be grateful for any amendments.

What I can be relatively sure of is the general influences on my work. In addition to my theatre training at the American Conservatory Theatre in San Francisco, Circle in the Square in New York City, National Youth Theatre in London and New York University, where I received my Bachelor of Fine Arts degree, I have been fortunate enough to study improvisation in a variety of schools. The improv content of this book is drawn from three major sources:

- Keith Johnstone and the Theatresports companies around the world. Theatresports is an improv format in which teams of improvisers compete for the approval of Olympic-style judges. Johnstone created it to bring the excitement and audience involvement of sporting events to the theatre. Johnstone's book, *Impro* (1979), is an improv 'bible' and the Theatresports communities around the world continue to build on his work.

- Del Close and the Chicago schools. Del Close was a director at Second City, and later the founder of ImprovOlympic. Second City is perhaps the most famous comedy and improv company in the States, spawning such talents as John Belushi, Bill Murray, Mike Nichols and Elaine May, and scores of others. Close's philosophies have been recorded in *Truth in Comedy* (Halpern, Close and Johnson, 1994). As a student at Chicago City Limits in New York, I became one of many students who have inherited the work of Close, Paul Sills and others who developed the improv lexicon in Chicago.
- Viola Spolin, whose book, *Improvisation for the Theater* (1983), was instrumental in the modern-day improv movement in the United States.

One note. It is a rare business community that has not met this work with some initial scepticism. Inviting the world of theatre into business can be risky stuff. It is certainly not part of most traditional business environments. The objections tend to take a similar form regardless of the country or industry. 'I think this is a wonderful approach,' a client will say, 'but our employees will not take to it.' 'Engineers/the Japanese/accountants/the French do not like to learn this way.' Inevitably, the decision makers question the willingness of the participants to engage in these activities. However, across all of the job descriptions and cultures we have experienced, with only very few individual exceptions, the class participants responded positively. As long as the contextual value was articulated and the cultural norms respected, participants seem not only to enjoy but also to see value in the work.

Finally, the power of theatre as a training tool resides in its experiential nature – its ability to connect people to their intuition, their bodies, their intellect and each other. Our hope is that the practices in *Training Using Drama* will be engaged in, not just read about, and that modification or ultimate rejection will be made after, not before, the concepts are explored. But first things first. Here we go.

Section 1

1
The principles of improv

> We all [improvise] everyday – none of us goes through our day to day life
> with a script to tell us what to do.
>
> Kim 'Howard' Johnson (Halpern, Close and Johnson, 1994)

'Hey, could you read this letter on stage?' the young man says. He proffers a
note written on lined ring-binder paper. 'I want to propose to my girlfriend
tonight. I thought you could read this to her on stage, and ask her to marry
me.'

'Yes, if you like,' Kenn, an improvisational actor scheduled to introduce
the evening's show, responds. He is experienced and confident. The code
says, 'Make the audience happy.' Plus, the assignment sounds great.
Romantic. Exciting. Good theatre.

Half an hour later Kenn is on his knees in front of the proposee. With the
urging of her boyfriend, she has volunteered to come up on stage, where
she has played a scene with Kenn. They are now at the top of an imaginary
hill, resting their legs after an imaginary bike ride. She is being proposed to
by proxy. Kenn reads the letter.

'Kelly,' it says, 'you are the most beautiful woman I've ever met. I love the
way you care for people and are so generous and kind. I would like to share
the rest of my life with you. Will you marry me?'

There is a pause. 'Well?' Kenn says.

'Uh…' For a moment the woman is unsure. Is this real? She looks out at
the audience.

'I need an answer,' Kenn says, the tickle of panic beginning at his scalp.

'Uh… no,' Kelly responds.

At this point, most of us would probably have cut our losses and, embarrassed for ourselves and the less-than-blissful couple, ushered the woman
to her seat. Not so with Kenn. He was committed. He was going to accept
whatever the woman said and continue with the scene. As if it were himself
he was fighting for, he persisted.

'No? Why not?' he says.

'I just don't feel that way about you,' she says to Kenn, caught up herself in the role-play.

'Is there someone else?' he asks. The improvisers cringe backstage and look around for a vaudeville hook.

'Yes,' she says. The woman says 'Yes' in front of an audience of strangers!

'Who?' Kenn asks.

'This guy at the gym,' she says.

'What's his name?' Kenn astonishingly pursues.

'Hank,' she replies.

Improvisational actors – improvisers – make up scenes, songs, stories, entire plays, on the spot, with no script or planned scenarios. They work collaboratively in front of paying customers who expect to be entertained and amazed, with only their skills, philosophies and colleagues to guide them. Sometimes the results seem magical. Sometimes they feel disastrous. Only through the willingness to risk failure, though, are improvisers able to delight audiences with their successes. The secret, which improvisers know, is that the 'failures' – as in the scene above – can be as satisfying and useful as the successes.

Does the job of an improviser sound familiar? Not so different from everyday life, is it? Rather like surviving in the contemporary business culture. Increasingly, the corporate world is looking like the world of improvisational theatre. The script is constantly being reinvented. The opportunities to plan deeply before acting are becoming fewer, shorter and less reliable. Not coincidentally, in recent years businesses have begun to realize the value of consciously fostering creativity and teamwork within their organizations. The techniques, philosophies and exercise of improvisation, then, are a rich source of learning for them.

Many of the current experiential kinds of training games have their origin in the world of improv. But improv has more to offer than just fun activities to break up the monotony of lectures. (Not that breaking up monotonous training is unimportant.) Trainers must have good performance skills. Sivasailam Thiagarajan (Thiagi), the great guru of training games, says that he believes there is no better preparation for becoming a trainer than acting. Trainers must have excellent presentations skills, as well as the flexibility to sense a group's needs and respond in the moment. As creativity and communication skills – teamwork, coaching, leadership, idea generation – continue to be increasingly in demand, trainers can tap the world of improv for content-related exercises. Many improv techniques and games are 'frame' games that can be used to enhance learning, regardless of the specific content. Improv activities have been used in training as varied as product training, induction courses, technical training and diversity workshops. To summarize, improv can be used:

- to develop the personal skills of trainers;
- to enhance the creativity and communication skills of managers and individual contributors;
- to increase the effective delivery of virtually any course content.

Here's why. In order for improvisers to accomplish their potentially daunting task – creating on the spot, collaboratively, in front of a paying public – they have developed a set of approaches and agreements designed to create a culture of innovation and collaboration. They have a head start in training individuals to be successful in an ever-changing, highly collaborative environment. Improv exercises can be wonderful 'jolts', introducing individuals to new ways of thinking, as well as wonderful workout routines for exercising the muscles of creativity and teamwork.

Often people ask how improvisers can 'rehearse' if they don't know what is going to happen in a show. Like athletes, improvisers practise skills that can be utilized in a variety of situations. They work on expanding and strengthening their abilities, even though they do not know what the specific events will be in an individual game. The fundamental skills that improvisers develop are:

- trust;
- spontaneity;
- accepting offers;
- listening and awareness;
- storytelling;
- non-verbal communication.

Let's take a look at what these entail and how they might apply to the workplace.

Trust

The heart of collaboration is trust. Without it no oratory will be convincing, no agreement solid, no relationship productive. This truth is evident to the improviser, as it is to police or army partners. When you willingly walk into danger with nothing but your colleagues to protect you, you had better trust them. Perhaps it is a little extreme to compare performers to military personnel at war. I certainly would not want to diminish the bravery and importance of those men and women. But improv certainly feels danger-ous. So improvisers demand that they have colleagues whom they can trust, and they have developed exercises (and tests) to build it.

Team members in any field can use these activities. Sometimes the work-place can feel like a war zone, too. Competition is rampant; casualties are reported every day; daring acts of bravery are required. It is no longer enough to be on the 'leading edge'. Now we aim to live on the 'bleeding edge'. Imagine, then, how important it is for leaders, managers and trainers to create an environment of trust when they are virtually sending their people into battle.

Spontaneity

From a very early age, most of us are taught to censor ourselves. Good thing, really. Without the ability to control our impulses, make judgements and choose when and if to act, we would be crippled. We could not learn to read, eat with utensils or shed our nappies. Civilization itself is a set of agreed-upon limits we place on our uncensored actions. However, there is a price. We spend so much time exercising our judgement muscles that our creativity muscles can atrophy.

In order to create, a person needs to trust his or her impulses and follow through on seemingly irrational, non-linear or 'foolish' ideas. While the abilities to evaluate and analyse are important, if they are out of balance with our abilities to brainstorm and take risks, creativity is sadly impeded.

In improv, there is no time to evaluate. By definition, improvisation is creating in the moment without the ability to revise. Improvisers practise getting out of their own way so that they can recognize and utilize their innovative ideas. What is especially interesting about unleashing one's impulses is that it is often the ideas that seem the most dangerous or the most obvious – the ones that our rational mind would have us censor – that yield the greatest fruit. If Kenn, in the scene recounted above, had followed socially acceptable restraint and refrained from questioning his audience volunteer, everyone might have been more comfortable, but the resulting scene would have been much less compelling and memorable.

Accepting offers

When we practise being spontaneous, we learn to accept our own ideas. It is equally important to accept others' ideas. Teamwork of any sort depends on both our ability and our willingness to do that. In improv, ideas and actions

– words, physical actions, character attributions, musical accompaniments, lines of dialogue – are called 'offers'. Anything your partner does or says is an offer. In a moment, an improviser can accept or reject a myriad of offers. Improvisers learn early that if you do not accept whatever is offered to you, you can spend loads of time searching around for something better and never get anywhere. All you have when you are improvising is the current offers. There is no other plan or guideposts. Nothing else exists.

The correlated truth in business is more applicable than one might expect. Often, organizations lose speed and opportunities because ideas are rejected (or merely nominally accepted). Saying 'Yes' sounds good, but can be hard in practice. People reject ideas without fully exploring them all the time, for many reasons. New ideas may mean more work; people fear that someone else will get more credit; the idea feels risky; people think they have a 'better' idea of their own. However, every time we say 'No' to an idea instead of 'Yes', an opportunity is lost. That does not mean, of course, that evaluation is not useful or that we should commit to every idea. When we depend on our judgement muscles exclusively, though, we throw the baby out with the bathwater, the electricity out with the light bulb.

There is another step to accepting offers in the improv world. Just saying 'Yes', as powerful as it is, is not enough. Improvisers live and die by the 'Yes, and…' rule. 'Yes, and…' means that not only must I, the improviser, accept an offer, I must build on it. I must contribute. I must make an offer of my own in response to my partner's. It is this process that harnesses the power of collaboration. Everyone offers and accepts. Each team member is responsible for both contributing to and supporting the group's activity. Through the implementation of this method, brainstorming sessions lead to innovative solutions. Even the smallest spark can be fanned into illuminating flames.

Listening and awareness

It is impossible to accept and build on others' ideas if we cannot recognize them. By enhancing listening and observation skills, teams and individuals can harvest significantly more ideas, increase their understanding of each other and communicate more effectively.

Improvisers have the pressure of having to listen and react in front of an audience. They worry about not only what they must say next, but how they will look, how people will judge them and not falling off the stage. These concerns diminish the ability to sense and build on offers. The feelings improvisers can have on stage – self-consciousness, pressure to get things right, not wanting to make a fool of themselves – are different only in intensity, not in kind, to the pressures that many of us feel most of the time. So many internal and external realities vie for our attention. Keith Johnstone, the founder of Theatresports, and a beloved and admired improv teacher, dedicates much of his work to combating the fear that can blind performers to offers that are terribly obvious to passive observers.

Most people are both more and less aware than they think they are. We take in an extraordinary amount of information that we ignore and, at the same time, our inability really to pay attention can confound our sincerest attempts to communicate. The good news is that listening and general awareness are muscles. They can be developed and exercised.

Storytelling

Why is narrative so important? All communication, it can be argued, is storytelling. The way humans make sense of facts is by creating narratives that link bits of data to each other and to past experiences. Audiences, then, are constantly looking for stories to help them understand the information being presented to them, and to keep them interested. As long as audiences are wondering, 'What happens next?', they will continue to watch.

Audiences may leave a performance remembering a funny line, but the improviser who uttered it will tell you that it was the team's ability to create a compelling narrative that sustained the show. Lots of the climactic moments that audiences remember are only satisfying because of the context surrounding them, many of the characters only defined and adored because of the situation in which they behaved. Charna Halpern and Del Close, the great Chicago improv guru, say, 'The most direct path to disaster in improvisation is to make jokes' (Halpern, Close and Johnson, 1994).

Like candyfloss, an improv show with gags and no stories can be delicious for a bit, but quickly becomes unfulfilling. Among other things, if you are going to present an entire evening of jokes – as many stand-ups do – they had better be really, really good jokes. That is why comedians can spend years perfecting a single line. Improv, of course, does not provide that opportunity. *Whose Line Is It Anyway?*, the popular British, and later US, improvised television show seems to get away with quick, jokey improv. However, most theatre audiences demand a narrative in order to stay engaged. Even *Whose Line Is It Anyway?* adds a mock competition to provide some narrative structure for each episode. In an attempt to offer their audiences (and themselves) turkey dinners in lieu of candyfloss, many of the most respected live improv companies have turned to new show formats that allow them to create performances with longer, more complex story-lines. And even within the most traditional 'short-form' structures, story-telling opportunities are increasingly sought after.

The power of story can be harnessed with great success by trainers and managers, too. By incorporating storytelling activities, a trainer can support the unconscious process of story creation, thereby enhancing the partici-pants' attention and ability to retain information. Storytelling can be used for everything from increasing presentation skills to building teams to reviewing technical processes to motivating employees.

Non-verbal communication

Everyone knows that there is much more to being a good communicator than the words we use. A sneer, a peek at a watch, sweat, all can have more impact than the content of the arguments. That is why so many corporate executives have begun to hire media trainers. A tilt of the head, an 'um' or an 'ah', a smile can indicate trustworthiness, dishonesty, interest or apathy. Unlike those of books, our external covers can offer many reliable clues to our inner natures. That said, much of our physical and vocal behaviour is learnt. Therefore, we can acquire and modify our communication habits to become more effective and more versatile communicators.

Who are the experts in this process? Actors, of course. Their job is to portray 'characters' – human beings, animals, spirits – potentially very different from themselves. So actors study how internally and externally to expand their range of behaviours to communicate a wide variety of feelings and ideas in a wide variety of styles and contexts. Lay people, too, can prac-tise flexing and strengthening their physical and vocal repertoire.

Perhaps 'judging a book by its cover' is not quite as superficial as the phrase might suggest. Just as our subconscious is evident in our dreams, so it reveals itself in our bodies. There are lots of exercises actors use to increase their ability to be heard, to be relaxed in front of people and to support their content with their tone of voice and physical expression. Without these abilities, no matter how good they are at making verbal offers, performers will be unable to convey a variety of characters or convince an audience of their authenticity.

An interesting subset of the behaviours (non-verbal and verbal) that improvisers explore and play with falls under the heading of 'status'. Johnstone, in his seminal work *Impro* (1979), devotes a substantial section to the topic. Exercises designed to recognize and manipulate status behaviours have become some of the most enlightening and useful tech-niques to translate into business settings.

As improvisation is such a rich source of creativity and collaboration techniques, it is not surprising that companies have begun to tap it as a source of training and inspiration. The following chapters will offer ideas, exercises, tips and techniques designed to allow any interested party to glean value from this body of work.

Just say 'Yes'.

2
Trust

Sky diving without a parachute is suicide. Total freedom is suicide… Holing up in a closet is vegetating. Total security is vegetating.

Gordon MacKenzie (1996)

The principle

There is a statistic, perhaps apocryphal, that has floated around for years, which says that people are more afraid of public speaking than they are of death. Recently, a workshop participant pointed out that this may be because public speaking seems, for most of us, more imminent. When it comes down to it, we might prefer to get up in front of people and talk than meet our maker. But research does point to the fact that getting up in front of others and expressing ourselves can cause extreme amounts of stress. When we are presenting with a team, then, we had better trust the people on stage with us.

Diane Rachel, a coach and performer with Bay Area Theatresports offers an improv course entitled 'Sex and violence'. It is designed to get students comfortable doing scenes that include the most taboo and dangerous subject matter. Why? Because taboo and dangerous subject matter is the stuff of great theatre. The title of her course provokes deliberately. In actuality, the shows at Bay Area Theatresports tend almost exclusively toward mainstream family entertainment. Sex might consist of a big hug or a tame smooch. Violence is usually depicted in slow motion with imaginary weapons or punches thrown from a few feet away. Still, even these relatively mild actions can excite audiences and intimidate performers. When it comes down to it, Rachel's class is mostly about building trust among a group of performers. Trust grows through acknowledging discomfort, establishing and enforcing ground rules, and engaging in the activity together. The last, actually participating, makes the real difference. Ultimately, the only way to engender trust is to show, through your actions, that you are trustworthy. The only way to do that is to act.

That does not mean that you must wait until the moment of crisis – a fire, a war, a performance, a sales call – to build trust. There are plenty of small cues that people read in order to assess whether their team-mates and managers should be trusted. Every action, every word, whether directed at us or at those around us, gives us a clue to the trustworthiness of our colleagues. Much of improv rehearsal time focuses on creating trust – helping individuals become more focused and empathetic, and providing the group members with opportunities to build rapport.

The trust formula

John Phillips of Synectics suggested the following formula to define trust:

$$\text{Trust} f \frac{(\text{credibility})(\text{intimacy})}{\text{risk}}$$

Credibility is defined as competence – possessing the knowledge, skills and abilities necessary for the task. Intimacy, in this context, translates to empathy, the capability to understand, identify with and care for others. When people believe that someone possesses these two qualities, their trust for that person will increase. The last piece of the formula states that the higher the perceived level of risk, the more credibility and intimacy are needed to engender trust.

In business, a lot of attention can be focused on credibility. How well does this person perform? How much does he or she know? For trainers, credibility is gained through subject-matter knowledge and group process skills. If trainers have no experience in a given industry, that community may question them more. Similarly, if their flip charts are illegible, their capability may be doubted. In both cases, credibility feels easy to measure and to increase through training and experience.

Intimacy, at first glance, seems harder to develop. Isn't empathy just a personality trait that some people possess or something that happens naturally with time? Improvisers believe that empathy is a skill. And they have devised exercises to cultivate it.

In *To Kill a Mockingbird*, Harper Lee's classic novel of life in a small town in the southern United States, Atticus Finch says to his six-year-old daughter, 'You just learn a single trick, Scout, you'll get along better with all kinds of folks… You never really understand a person till you consider things from his point of view… Till you climb inside of his skin and walk around in it.' That is a pretty good definition of empathy. It could also define the acting process. Actors learn how to identify with characters and get inside their skins, so to speak. The further they are from the character, the better. Many actors love to play villains, because the 'bad guys' are often the more complex and intriguing characters. Interestingly, actors will often say that they do not see their villain personas as evil at all. Once they have understood the pain and motivations of their characters, no matter how vile we may think those characters are, the actors speak of them with affection.

Getting to know each other

The same phenomenon happens in real life. The better we know each other, the greater the chance we will empathize. So a good first step to building trust is to provide opportunities for the team members to learn about each other. For example, ask a team to exchange the stories behind their names – first name, last name, nickname. For example, 'Kat' is short for 'Katherine'. I got the name 'Katherine' because my mother had always been told she looked strikingly like the film star, Katharine Hepburn. 'Koppett' is a name my father made up. He was born in Russia and, when he became a sportswriter in the 50s, he changed his name to 'Koppett' because our original family name, 'Kopeliovitch', was constantly mispronounced. And, he said, it wouldn't fit on the newspaper's byline. This simple exercise spurs conversation and reveals details that individuals usually have not shared. Especially in countries with diverse populations, names can reveal deep and varied histories. As innocuous as they may seem, these small bits of information begin to weave a net of safety and connection that allows empathy to grow and trust to develop.

Story of your name

Overview:
- Participants share the story of how they got their names.

Improv topics:
- Trust
- Storytelling

Purposes:
- Ice-breaker
- Warm-up
- Team building
- Communication

Supplies:
- None

Time:
- Approximately 1–2 minutes per participant

Number of players:
- Variable

Game flow:
- Have each participant share the story of his or her name.
- Let participants know that they can tell the story of their first name, last name, a nickname, whatever they like.
- Some facilitators like to add that participants can lie if they like. This takes the onus off people who do not wish to share, or feel as if they do not have a story to tell.
- Model the process by going first.
- Let the speaker pick the next speaker.

Variations:
- If the group is too large for everyone to participate in the allotted amount of time, split the group into sub-groups. Sub-groups of 6–10 are ideal.

Tips:
- Set a time limit of one minute if you have a large group or not a lot of time. People may find they can talk about themselves for a long time.

- If people say they have absolutely no story about their name, you might prompt them to talk about how they feel about their name, or what name they wanted to have as a child.

Suggested debrief questions:
- What is the value of learning non-work-related information about each other?
- Did you discover anything about yourself that you didn't know?
- What did you learn about the group in general?
- In what ways do you feel different from how you felt before we began the exercise?
- What effect does hearing a personal story have?
- How does it feel to share a personal story?

Source:
- Bay Area Theatresports, via George Silides' ice-breaking activities for pastors.

Another getting-to-know-each-other activity, 'Stats', which I originally learnt from Bay Area Theatresports, is a variation on musical chairs. Everyone sits in a circle, with one chair-less person standing in the centre. That person shouts out a fact about him- or herself and everyone to whom that fact also applies must get up and find a new chair. Those are the only rules. (And that no one gets hurt.) I have found that this simple game produces great delight. There are a couple of wonderful things about it. First, it creates an environment in which the participants themselves control what they reveal about themselves and decide what they wish to learn about others. Second, the exercise is designed so that it is not the most aggressive or most vocal people who are in control. In fact, it may turn out that the more retiring team members find themselves in the centre of the circle more. This enables those who might not otherwise have a voice to lead the discussion.

Stats

Overview:
- A musical-chairs-like game in which participants exchange titbits of information about themselves and find out what they have in common.

Improv topics:
- Trust
- Spontaneity

Purposes:
- Ice-breaker
- Warm-up
- Energy builder
- Team building
- Communication
- Needs assessment

Supplies:
- One chair per participant

Time:
- 15–30 minutes

Number of players:
- 6–20 per circle

Game flow:
- Arrange a circle of chairs, one for each participant.
- Stand in the centre of the circle.
- State the following rules:
  - Whoever is standing in the centre shouts out the next 'stat'.
  - Each statistic must be true of the person who says it.
  - If that statistic is true of you, find a new chair.
  - *No one gets hurt.*
- Offer the first statistic.
- Play along (if you are not playing, make sure the number of chairs is one smaller than the number of participants, and have one volunteer start in the middle).
- Play for however long you wish. You may give a three-minute or three-round warning if you like.

Variations:
- Use as a needs analysis or more focused content activity by limiting the types of statements (eg the statements must involve sales experiences or the statements must be about your experiences with diversity).
- If you have a very large group or a space that will not accommodate a circle of chairs, you may play 'Roaming stats'. For this version:
  - Follow the general rules above, but instead of having the participants find new chairs, have the speaker instruct participants to go to a certain part of the room (eg over in the corner; behind the table; at the far wall).
  - Whoever wishes to shout out the next statistic is free to do so.

  Additional advantages of this version are:

  - The group can see who fits into each category more easily.
  - It is less physically demanding.
  - The flow is more free-form, so that anyone with an idea has the opportunity to shout it out.

Tips:
- Check with participants about any physical limitations. I have had participants on crutches or in wheelchairs play by touching the chair with a hand or crutch. And pregnant women have enjoyed the game, too. Still, you must get agreement ahead of time.

Suggested debrief questions:
- What did you find out that surprised you?
- What did you share that surprised you?
- What is the value of playing this game?
- Why do we censor ourselves?
- What would you like to change about your interactions based on this experience?

Source:
- Bay Area Theatresports, Ruth Zapora and Patricia Ryan

Make your partner look good

Getting to know each other makes it more likely that we will not only pay attention to each other, but that we will support each other. 'Make your partner look good' is an improv mantra. It means concentrating on your partner rather than on yourself and taking responsibility for both of you. 'If your partner drops the ball,' we say, 'it is *your* responsibility, not your partner's.' What a difference when team members interact this way. 'Ball toss' illustrates the concept physically. Participants stand in a circle and toss a ball in a repeated pattern so that each person receives and throws the ball once. Once the pattern is established, the facilitator adds more and more balls, increasing the level of difficulty. Finally, the participants are instructed to walk around randomly while maintaining the same pattern. At first, groups struggle. Team members throw balls without looking to see if their partner is ready. People blame each other for dropping balls. Sometimes, participants try to confuse each other by throwing especially fast or high. However, when the facilitator tells them that the *thrower* is responsible if the ball does not get caught, things change. People focus on their partners rather than themselves. They make eye contact before tossing the balls. They aim and throw gently. They call each other's names to get their partner's attention. The concept of accountability gets bandied about these days. Ironically, the conversation often consists of admonitions directed at others, as in '*You* should be more accountable.' Thinking always of making your partner look good is a way to separate true accountability from thinly disguised blame.

Participants from Western cultures tend to find the collaborative aspect of 'Ball toss' especially challenging. It seems their competitive training can leave them prone to winging balls at each other's heads. My Asian participants, on the other hand, seem more inclined to watch out for, and take care of, their partners. What do you think? Does your culture – national or business – value competition or collaboration more? Individual or team achievement?

Ball toss

Overview:
- Participants throw a series of balls around in a set pattern, adding as many balls as they can. Eventually, the group can break out of the circle, and additional objectives may be added.

Improv topics:
- Trust
- Accepting offers
- Listening and awareness

Purpose:
- Ice-breaker
- Warm-up
- Energy builder
- Team building
- Communication
- Closing

Supplies:
- 5–10 soft juggling balls or sacks

Time:
- 10–30 minutes

Number of players:
- 6–20

Game flow:
- Have the participants stand in a circle.
- One person throws the ball to someone across the circle.
- That person puts a hand on his or her head to indicate that he or she has been thrown to, and then throws the ball to someone else across the circle. This pattern continues till everyone has thrown and received the ball once.
- Then the pattern is repeated with each participant continuing to throw and receive from the same person each time.
- As the team improves, the leader adds more and more balls.
- After the pattern is established and a number of balls are in play, ask the group members to walk randomly around the room, continuing to throw and receive from the same people.

- Finally, play different rounds, asking the participants to achieve different objectives. These objectives may include:
  - never drop a ball;
  - throw the balls as quickly as possible;
  - throw the ball as far as possible.

Variations:
- Play passing various objects – a ball, a frisbee, a beach ball, a chair (which should be passed, not thrown).
- Play with different objects being passed in different patterns.

Tips:
- Make sure the group remembers the original pattern before adding objects.
- Remind the group that the objective is to make the other people look good. Tell them that if their partner drops the ball, it is their responsibility.
- Remind the group of the 'no-one-gets-hurt' rule. Use soft objects or require that a heavier object (like a chair) is passed, not thrown.
- As a final round, you may ask the participants to choose a private, individual objective and see what happens.

Suggested debrief questions:
- What helped us achieve our task?
- What stood in the way?
- What happened when I suggested that it was your responsibility to ensure that your partner caught the ball?
- What effect did changing the specific objectives have?
- How is this like real-life teamwork?

Source:
- Rebecca Stockley

Earlier in the chapter we talked about how Diane Rachel built trust by acknowledging discomfort, establishing and enforcing ground rules, and having her students practise together. Using improv games, it is possible to see trust improve before your eyes. For example, the use of an 'ice-breaker' admits that there is ice to be broken – it acknowledges discomfort. Games of all sorts provide a structure or set of rules within which people can play with security – they set ground rules. And the more you play, the more comfortable people become – games work as practice for higher-risk situations.

It cannot be said too often: whether in the context of daily inter-personal activity or in a workshop setting, trust is the foundation upon which everything rests. If you wish workshop participants or team members to make themselves vulnerable, you must nurture their efforts regardless of the outcome. The following chapters present a variety of concepts, all of which are capable of enhancing creativity and teamwork. None of them will amount to anything unless the environment is imbued with trust.

Application

As trainers, managers and leaders, we require people to follow our advice and procedures. In order to be effective, we must be deemed trustworthy. Although specific behaviours may vary depending on the cultural context, the underlying truth remains the same: trust is a necessary ingredient for creativity and collaboration to flourish. In addition to incorporating trust-building activities into our work, here are some ideas for enhancing trust.

Practise what you preach

The 'Do what I say not what I do' school of guidance has been shown to be ineffective. If you have enough authority, people might comply, but they will not trust you. If you encourage people to take risks and then punish them when they fail, they are even more unlikely to risk than if you had never brought up the topic.

A team-building consultant I know used to ask his employees to deliver parts of his training workshops as part of their professional development. 'This is your bit,' he would say. 'I trust you. Design it however you wish.' Then, when the moment came, he would interrupt and contradict them in front of the workshop participants. Needless to say, trust eroded very quickly. And the effect was only exacerbated when he spoke of trust the next time.

Recognize that you are seen

Human beings are highly attuned to potential danger, and they judge situations by what has happened to others before them. It is the monkey that saw the previous monkey eat the poisoned berry, and therefore avoided eating it himself, that survived. Every interaction affects not only the person whom it involves but also everyone who sees the event or hears the story.

In the example above, when the consultant undermined a trainer, he sabotaged not only the trainer's trust in him but the trust of the other employees. They heard the story and became nervous about training with him. The workshop participants also doubted the consultant. They saw what he was doing. If he was not going to support his own people, why should they believe him when he said they should take care of each other? And why should they feel safe to participate in his activities or to ask questions? It is frighteningly easy to build a reputation. Build the one you want.

Set expectations

If people are unclear about what it is you want of them, they can feel undermined, even when that is not your intention. The more straightforward you can be about the procedures and outcomes you expect, the more likely it is that people will succeed. You will not have to go back on your word. People will not feel confused or wrongly attacked if things veer off track. It is wonderful to offer people the freedom to create and problem-solve in their own way. However, if there are specific results you are looking for, you had better explain them from the beginning. Perhaps if the consultant above had set more specific expectations of his trainers, for example, he would not have felt the need to jump in during the workshop.

Frame your intentions

We are aware of our intentions, whereas others can only guess them based on our behaviours. By 'framing' or setting context for our actions, we may avoid mistrust born of misinterpretation. Studies of attribution theory show that people will forgive harmful actions if they believe the intentions were honourable. For example, if I arrive late to a meeting, other attendees may assume that I do not think their time is valuable. Or they may assume I am unreliable. If I let them know that I was in a car accident or, less dramatically, if I apologize for keeping everyone waiting and let them know that I respect them and their schedules, I can mitigate the damage. That does not mean that actions will be excused time and time again, but in individual instances sharing your intentions can avert the erosion of trust. Let people know why you are requesting something. Tell them why you made a particular decision. Articulate the need, as you see it, for whatever process you have employed.

Provide low-risk opportunities

If you ask people to take huge risks without establishing yourself as dependable, you are likely to be rebuffed. Find small ways to reassure people before you embark on high-risk activities. As mentioned, games are tools for accomplishing this task. Another technique is to have one-to-one conversations with those you are coaching – conversations devoted solely to uncovering their needs and concerns. Let people know you are willing to listen before you ask them to listen in return. Yet another strategy is to give people easy tasks that they feel comfortable with before challenging them, so that they can trust their own competence and you can trust your ability to be supportive.

Choose your activities carefully

Some of the most powerful training activities are called 'jolts'. A jolt is an experience that dramatically challenges a participant's attitudes or beliefs. Jolts can be designed and used in training situations to great effect. They can also leave participants feeling vulnerable, manipulated or betrayed. In choosing to use these kinds of activities, weigh the pay-off against the price. As with a physician, a trainer's responsibility is first to do no harm. Sometimes a trainer chooses an activity not because it is the best way to facilitate learning but because he or she enjoys the ease or status that accompanies running it. Be clear about why you are employing an activity that requires manipulation. Is it necessary consciously to mislead the group or set them up to fail? Can you get the same value from a less confrontational experience? Remember, trust is even harder to rebuild than to build.

Key points

- Trust is the foundation for all creative and collaborative endeavours.
- To establish trust:
    - acknowledge discomfort;
    - establish and follow ground rules;
    - practise together.
- Trust f (credibility)(intimacy)/risk.
- Make your partner look good.
- Practise what you preach.
- Recognize that you are seen.
- Set expectations.
- Frame your intentions.
- Provide low-risk opportunities.
- Choose your activities carefully.

3

Spontaneity

Spontaneity is the moment of personal freedom when we are faced with a reality and see it, explore it, and act accordingly.

Viola Spolin (1983)

The principle

One of the staples of improv training is a game called 'Invisible balls' (see page 32). The exercise is taught in every beginning improv class, played as a warm-up in virtually all improv companies and utilized in creativity workshops around the world. In 'Invisible balls', the participants stand in a circle and throw an imaginary ball back and forth. Each time participants toss the ball, they make a sound. Their partners, the people to whom they have thrown the ball, repeat the sound as they catch it. There are no rules about what kind of sound to make, no stipulations about what sounds are acceptable or prohibited. Anything goes.

At first, learners often express a surprising amount of discomfort playing 'Invisible balls'. After all, there is no real ball, so one need not be coordinated. The exercise demands no specific sounds, so one cannot fail. But regardless of the lack of skill required or of rules of right and wrong, people find all sorts of ways to evaluate their input.

'How many people worried about creating a "good" sound?' the facilitator asks. At least half the participants raise their hand.

'How many thought that one or more of the sounds they made were "bad"?' Almost as many indicate agreement.

'Who felt that someone else made a better sound than they did?' Everyone laughs and nods.

'What were some of the reasons you judged your sounds as bad?' the facilitator probes.

The participants pipe up. 'It was too soft.' 'It had too many consonants.' 'It was too similar to the sound I made the first time.' 'It wasn't interesting.'

'Invisible balls' is a compelling game, because it highlights the arbitrary nature of our judgements. Usually, when we evaluate a product or an idea, we feel we have substantial reasons for doing so. We would love to say 'Yes' and follow our impulses, but they are wrong! The idea is just bad! However, even when we remove the semblance of content, our censoring voices can remain. 'Invisible balls' illustrates how capricious our internal judge can be.

Invisible balls

Overview:
- In a circle, participants throw invisible balls accompanied by sounds. The first person tosses the ball and makes a sound. The second person catches the ball and mimics the same sound. The second person then throws the ball to another person, making a new sound, which is repeated by the receiver. Eventually, more that one ball can be passed around the circle at the same time.

Improv topics:
- Trust
- Spontaneity
- Accepting offers
- Listening and awareness
- Non-verbal behaviour

Purpose:
- Ice-breaker
- Warm-up
- Energy builder
- Team building
- Creativity
- Communication

Supplies:
- Invisible balls (none)

Time:
- 5–20 minutes

Number of players:
- 4–20 per group

Game flow:
- Form a circle.
- Explain that you have an invisible ball. Toss it to someone and have him or her catch it. Then have the person throw it back to you.
- Further explain that the ball makes a sound. This time throw the ball with a sound – 'whee-ee'. Coach the receiver to repeat the sound.
- Have that person throw the ball to someone else with a new sound, which is echoed by the receiver, and so on.

- After the group has tossed the ball for a while, ask for feedback – 'How do you feel?' 'Are you censoring yourselves?' 'Why?'
- Continue the game adding more balls.
- Debrief.

Variations:
- Play with words instead of sounds.
- Play with sensory images (eg the smell of grass, a wet puppy tongue licking your face).
- Play with shared images – one person throws the first half and the second catches the completion. (Eg *Person A: 'A really high skyscraper...'* Person B: '...with a gorilla standing on the top.')
- Play with the thrower mouthing the words, and the receiver articulating out loud what he or she understood the first person to say.

Tips:
- Keep up a fast pace. Speed will help participants bypass their censors.
- Be willing to play along and make silly or ordinary sounds yourself.

Suggested debrief questions:
- Are you censoring yourselves? How? What were some of the judgements you made?
- Did anyone plan his or her sounds ahead of time? Why?
- Did anyone compare his or her sounds to other people's sounds?
- What does this tell us about our tendencies to censor in real life?
- How does this relate to creativity and idea generation?
- How did your experience change as the game continued?
- How did your experience change as more balls were added?

Source:
- Adapted from Viola Spolin, Chicago City Limits, Fratelli Bologna, Theatresports and Patricia Ryan

Learning to identify and follow impulses is the foundation of creativity. Virtually all literature on initiating the creative process counsels this: find ways to stimulate yourself and then spew forth ideas without evaluation. There will always be time to edit later. Julia Cameron, in *The Artist's Way* (1992), recommends that those who wish to be more creative write three pages of uncensored, unshared prose each morning. Anne Lamott, in her spirited and supportive book on writing, *Bird by Bird*, encourages 'shitty first drafts' (1994: 21–22). Business consultants and creativity experts all talk about separating idea generation from evaluation, about engaging in divergent processes before converging on a solution. The road to increased creative output is simple and well known. Embracing spontaneity in practice, though, can be a struggle.

In most cultures, we are trained from the earliest of ages to resist our impulses. My mother tells the story of how, as a young infant, I would cry whenever she put me down and left the room – until one day, on the advice of her doctor, she let me cry. My mother always ends the story the same way. 'I had to let you cry *once*! Once. And you never did it again.'

My mother was as attentive and concerned a parent as there has ever been. Still, for her sanity, she needed to teach me to repress my impulses. And I did. It is not so surprising to me that I learnt that lesson quickly. That's what babies do: learn. What is interesting to me is how proud my mother and I myself have been of this story. I became a 'good' baby. I didn't cry. I didn't demand. I followed the rules.

Most of us have some story about a parent or a teacher somehow discouraging our creative impulses. Johnstone (1979) railed against educational institutions in Britain for destroying innate creativity. He was not alone. How many of us have had the experience of being told we cannot sing, cannot draw or have no aptitude for a certain subject? Such statements are commonplace and they are self-fulfilling. The last 30 years have brought various new methods to the educational world, and individual creativity and self-esteem have been focused on in such movements as Montessori, founded in Italy, and the Nueva schools in the United States. However, many schools, from the United States to China, still spend more time on standardized tests, rote memorization and directive teaching styles than on developing creative thought and individual expression. It seems that we are ambivalent both about our capacity to teach creativity and teamwork, and about their innate value to begin with.

Resistance to spontaneity

In business settings, the same sorts of contradictions persist. Movements to support creativity have been growing in business, and yet there are many companies that resist. Why? Edward Deci, author of *Why We Do What We Do: Understanding self-motivation* (Deci and Flaste, 1996), asserts that motivation consists of three elements – a need for competence, a need for autonomy and a need for relatedness. Matthew Richter, my partner and a student of Deci's, has been working on applying their theories to the workplace. He advises (2001) that teamwork, empowerment and opportunities for self-expression result in higher worker satisfaction and therefore in higher productivity and retention. Ironically, though we know intellectually that spontaneity is desirable, actually being spontaneous can feel like a threat to all three of the important aspects of motivation noted above. If we do not evaluate our ideas before we articulate them, how can we have a sense of control, even over ourselves? If we do not know how and why we are responding in certain ways, how can we feel confident of our competence? If we are willing to think and act outside the generally agreed-upon ways in a situation, what guarantee do we have that we will be accepted?

Although many of us profess to dislike repression, when it comes down to it we are not sure we want more freedom. Johnstone claims, 'Most people I meet are secretly convinced that they're a little crazier than the average person' (1979). If that is what we believe, do we really want to let others in on the fact? If we, ourselves, were really free to do and speak and think, unfettered, then what would we learn about ourselves? What would we be compelled to follow through on? How would we know if we belonged?

In addition, some of us like the idea that creating is hard work – that only the most brilliant, tenacious and experienced individual can come up with the next best product or process. If spontaneously following our most ludicrous or most mundane whim is the way to success, then what kind of security do seniority and expertise offer?

An improv colleague of mine shared the following story illustrating the threatening aspect of spontaneous creation. We had just performed the opening night of a new, completely improvised musical format, *Spontaneous Broadway*. Her father, a classically trained musician, expressed both amazement and doubt about our show. 'You couldn't really have improvised all that,' he claimed. 'You must have planned the story. At least you already knew the music, right?' My friend had been improvising for years. Her father had heard about her endeavours for close to a decade. He had seen plenty of shows. But when he saw a group of improvisers succeed at creating songs with structure, rhyming lyrics, metaphors and melodies, he was dumbfounded. Composing was supposed to be difficult. If this ragtag group could do it on the spot, what did that say about him and his colleagues? How could he value his years of education and toil?

In other words, being spontaneous is both the most natural and the most difficult of behaviours. It is both delightful and risky. So, for trainers and managers in business settings, there are two questions: do we wish to foster spontaneity (ie creativity and autonomy) and, if so, what can we do to support it?

The case for spontaneity

I will assume for the moment that the answer to the first question is 'Yes'. The case for the increasing importance of creativity and self-motivation in the workplace due to accelerated time-frames, increased competition, and new markets and technologies has been documented repeatedly. For in-depth discussions of these topics, consult some of the texts in the 'References' and 'Further reading' sections. Let's discuss the second question: how can individuals and organizations become more spontaneous?

The following sections detail the improvisers' secrets for creating environments that foster spontaneity.

Spend time exercising the spontaneity muscle

Use warm-up exercises to get the juices flowing, before applying your creativity where it counts. Through games and exercises that are 'content-less', individuals can practise following their impulses while the stakes are low. For example, warm up before shows and play spontaneity games before idea-generation sessions.

Provide structure

Create a structure within which individuals can feel free to explore. As MacKenzie points out (1996), there are limits to the amount of freedom that is useful. Sometimes too few restrictions, even if the result is not actually dangerous, can inhibit creativity. Laura Livingston says that her job as the artistic director of Freestyle is to provide the jungle gym for the performers to swing on. To this end, many of the formats improvisers have developed set boundaries within which the improvisers must create. By limiting the options and focusing creative attention, improvisers can feel grounded and inspired, rather than unmoored. The limits themselves provoke ideas.

Do not censor

Just because we say we are in brainstorming mode, we do not automatically shut down our inner judge. The internalized voice of our parents, our teachers, our managers and our peers can be very strong. The most power-ful comment I ever heard regarding creative blocks came from Terry Sommer, my first improv teacher. She said, 'If you can't think of anything, it's because you're censoring what you're thinking of.' Sometimes, our internal judgements are so powerful that we stifle our impulses even before we are aware of them. We censor ourselves because we think we will be deemed inappropriate, stupid, silly or dull – if not by others, then by ourselves. In *Zen Mind, Beginner's Mind*, a book on Zen meditation and practice, Suzuki suggests that beginners are closer to the ultimate Zen state than practitioners who have been meditating for years, because they have no preconceptions about the right way to meditate or what their experience should be. He says, 'In the beginner's mind there are many possibilities, but in the expert's there are few' (1985).

There are some specific tips for bypassing your censor. One tip is to be foolish. Risk sounding silly. That's the whole point, really. For an idea to be creative, it must be somehow fresh, either in content or application. But ideas that are new, by definition, challenge the status quo. It is those ideas that are most likely to be dismissed. How many stories are there of a genius' ideas being rejected? Van Gogh sold one painting his entire lifetime; the Swiss scoffed at the crazy idea of digital watches; even Einstein scorned quantum theory.

As much as we say we value creativity, often what we mean is that we value the successful results of creative endeavours. People who create have a special gift. Not talent, I would offer – some do, some don't – but courage. If we are going to 'think outside the box', then, like a jack-in-the-box, we must pop out of one, not hunch protected inside.

Finally, let us look at the word 'foolish' itself. The fool in the archetypical sense is an innocent, with a childlike curiosity. The fool's power lies in a willingness to take risks. The universe protects fools as they take 'fool-ish' risks, indulge in sensual pleasures and discover new, exciting adventures. It was the fool in the royal courts who not only entertained the monarchs but also was able, through wit and charm, to tell truths that the most powerful advisers feared relaying. A willingness to be silly is the key to the fool's power and to our creative selves.

Another tip for bypassing your censor is to be obvious. Nothing will kill the creative process more quickly than trying to be 'creative', and trying to be 'interesting' is a surprisingly ineffective way to come up with original thoughts. When you search for something 'original' you reject idea after idea that pops into your head because it is obvious *to you*. 'Well, that's dull,' you think, or 'Everyone else must have already thought of this' or 'That was too easy; it must be stupid.' The truth is, what is obvious to you is the most organic, authentic impulse. That means it may also be the most valuable, since it is probably based on what is happening at the moment. By trusting the obvious and articulating it, there are two possibilities: either you are voicing something that everyone is thinking, but no one else has the courage to say (for example, the child who tells the emperor that he has no clothes); or something that seems very obvious to you, no one else has thought of.

An example of the latter is a legend at Freestyle Repertory Theatre. During a Theatresports performance, Laura Livingston and her team were challenged to a scene in which someone plays an inanimate object. Laura accepted the challenge and asked the audience for a location in which the scene could take place. Someone shouted out, 'A zoo.' Let's pause here. Take a moment to list all of the inanimate objects that come to mind. Got them? There are lots, right? Laura thought of something immediately. It was the only thing that came to mind. In fact, she was a little worried that if she didn't speak first, someone would take on the role of the only obvious choice and she would be left with nothing. She rushed to take her place and start the scene. What object did she choose to be? Monkey droppings. That's right, a monkey's excrement. Needless to say, no one else had thought of that particular object. But Laura swears it was absolutely the first and only thought in her head. The scene, by the way – between the monkey and the droppings – was very funny and rather sweet. And it was much more 'original' than whatever Laura might have come up with by rejecting her first idea as either too obvious or too tasteless.

Celebrate failure

In *The Art of Play*, a drama therapy text, Adam and Allee Blatner say, 'Permitting yourself to plunge into improvisation can be helpful by reminding yourself that in play there is endless room to make "mistakes"... Allow what might otherwise seem like a mistake to become transformed into an opportunity for further creativity' (1997). The only way to maximize creative risk is to celebrate the brave failure as well as the triumphant success. If failure is punished, then the risk of risking is just too high. Of course, there are times when following an innovative path will result in defeat. That defeat must be acknowledged and valued as a necessary cost of implementing the right process, or the process will be discarded with the result.

A favourite story that I have heard from a number of creativity consultants recounts how a vice-president at General Electric was summoned to chief executive officer Jack Welch's office after an innovative project of the VP's had failed miserably and cost the company over $10 million in one blow. The mortified employee handed Welch his resignation upon entering the office.

'What's this?' Welch asked.

'My resignation,' the VP replied.

'Your resignation!' Welch said. 'You can't resign. We just invested $10 million in your education.'

Now that's supporting failure.

The best part of embracing failure is that failure is not just a necessary evil. It can result in the most exciting ideas of all. Post-it™– notes are a famous example of a failed product. The chemists were trying to make a traditional adhesive, and their unsuccessful attempt led to the sticky substance that is strong enough to hold up the little squares of paper, yet can be attached and unattached at will. Alexander Graham Bell set out to create a hearing aid, and ended up with a phonograph. Improvisers speak of 'mistakes as gifts'. Sometimes failures can offer the greatest rewards. Of course, the same mistake made over and over out of laziness or stupidity benefits no one. But failures born of experimentation can be the stuff of magic.

The 'I failed!' activity primes the participants for celebrating the failures that signal risk and experimentation.

I failed!

Overview:
- Participants practise feeling comfortable while being silly and making mistakes by taking huge bows and proclaiming 'I failed!' or 'I made a mistake!' or 'I feel silly!' while the other participants cheer.

Improv topics:
- Spontaneity
- Trust

Purpose:
- Ice-breaker
- Warm-up
- Energy builder
- Team building
- Creativity
- Communication
- Problem solving

Supplies:
- None

Time:
- 2–5 minutes

Number of players:
- 2–200

Game flow:
- Have all the participants raise their hands above their heads, as a gymnast might after a routine.
- Ask them all to proclaim with relish and pride, 'I failed! I made a mistake! I feel stupid!'
- Then have them turn to someone next to them and take the position and state one of the phrases. Each person's partner cheers for the person, and then reciprocates.
- Finally, have the participants walk around the room to practise celebrating failure and applauding each other.

Variations:
- Have each person take a turn around the circle.
- Have participants play in groups of four or five.

Tips:
- Explain that it is only by making friends with failure that we will be willing to risk enough to succeed.
- This game is about acknowledging our discomfort and embracing it, rather than fleeing from it.
- Highlight for the participants that the phrases are 'I *feel* silly' and 'I *feel* stupid', not 'I *am* stupid.'

Source:
- Theatresports

Application

There are substantial pay-offs for increasing spontaneity in the workplace. The most direct application is to brainstorming. The concept of not censoring input during the divergent portion of idea-generation and problem-solving sessions has become commonplace. However, as we have discussed, offering up ideas without judgement is easier said than done. Trainers and facilitators can support the process in a number of ways. In addition, what many trainers and managers have already implemented in formal brainstorming sessions can be expanded to other aspects of their work.

Warm people up

Before asking people to generate content or learn new skills, engage them in warm-up activities. Through games like 'Invisible balls' (see page 32) or 'Word drill' (see page 191), participants can practise circumventing their censors in risk-free situations. Just like athletes stretch physical muscles before running, participants can warm up their creative muscles before focusing on a specific issue.

Warm-up activities can also prove valuable as a way to introduce experiential learning to communities that may be unfamiliar with it. Richter recently found himself delivering training at a nuclear power company. The workshop participants were used to rigid training methods, heavy on lecture and testing. In order to prepare them for his more experiential activities, Richter began the session with 'Stats' (see page 22). Activities like this set the stage for more interactive training, and let participants know what to expect.

Separate idea generation from idea evaluation

If you want to encourage spontaneity, especially in an atmosphere that generally has rules, processes and tangible measures of success (like the bottom line), you must create the space for ideas to be born and nurtured without testing and examining them too closely at first. Having officially sanctioned brainstorming sessions is one way to accomplish this. Another is to socialize with colleagues after hours at bars. You would be amazed how many show formats were created in these venues.

The opposite is also true. Evaluation is not a bad thing. If individuals feel that they will be stuck with crazy ideas, they will not share them. Assuring participants in brainstorming sessions that there will be time to examine and assess at another time will allow them to offer and accept wild ideas in the moment.

Remind people of the rules of brainstorming

When asking for ideas, reiterate the rules of brainstorming:

- No evaluation.
- Quantity over quality.
- Record ideas without discussion.
- Build on previous ideas.

Be vigilant about insisting that group members stick to them. As soon as someone begins to evaluate an idea, the safe space for generating risky ideas can be poisoned. If a group feels uncomfortable, it may try to censor individuals who are not censoring themselves.

Provide escape hatches

It is possible to devise ways for participants to abdicate responsibility for their ideas. This allows people to separate themselves from something that sounds foolish or risky, and therefore makes them more willing to share those ideas. The simplest method for detaching individuals from their ideas is to make the input anonymous. Have people write down ideas and post them. Have them write ideas on 3 × 5 cards and exchange them. Invite small groups to brainstorm and then share their ideas collectively. This technique has proved especially popular with our Japanese clients.

Another technique is to provide virtual 'masks' or substitute personas. For example, while brainstorming ideas for making meetings more effective, I have asked clients to think about what Mother Teresa might do were she running a meeting. Or Marcel Marceau. Or Mickey Mouse. Or the CEO of their company. Or their most eccentric relatives. In that context, participants can share ridiculous thoughts and say, 'Hey, I don't think that is a good idea, but Mickey Mouse might.' Other sorts of 'what-if' scenarios can be used to similar effect. 'What if it were the year 2020?' 'What if money were no object?' 'What if people had no hands?'

Assess needs

As managers and trainers we must allow people to voice confusion and resistance to our ideas. Otherwise we will not be able to gauge the real effect of our communication. Often, those are the kinds of thoughts that individuals may censor. When I taught English to Russian immigrants, my students would nod and assure me that they understood the lessons, even when they had no idea what I was talking about. They had been taught that the way to get by in school was to pretend to understand, to do publicly whatever the authority figure said to… and then to cheat. These tactics may have worked in terms of avoiding conflict or circumventing bureaucracy. They certainly did not help them learn. I found that I could help the students by saying, 'I will not continue until someone asks me a question.' Eventually, my students and I invented 'Stupid Simon'. Students would say, 'Kat, I do not have a question, but Stupid Simon would like to know…' (Stupid Simon became a virtual mask.)

Spontaneity games also work to gather needs. Many of the games we have discussed – 'Stats', 'Invisible balls' – can be modified to contain content. For instance, play 'Invisible balls' tossing 'the reasons you are here' or 'skills you expect to gain'.

As much as we have focused on the stress of spontaneity, spontaneous expression can feel exhilarating, too. Implementation of these tools and techniques will contribute not only effectiveness but joy to your work.

Behind the scenes

Being willing to be spontaneous is not an easy task, no matter how many years you spend working on it. The most experienced improvisers I know will admit that what has changed over the years is not that the little judging voices in their heads have gone away but that the improvisers have become more willing to ignore them. Even as I am writing about spontaneity, I notice how insistently the editor in my head judges what I write. It will not be assuaged by promises of later revisions or reminders that no one will have to see this draft. It plagues me. Here are just a few of the ways I am tempted to censor myself:

- 'You can't write that. It's too:
  - risqué;
  - obvious;
  - arty;
  - business-y;
  - literary;
  - clichéd;
  - American.'
- 'You can't include that. Your colleagues will:
  - disagree;
  - be jealous;
  - feel embarrassed;
  - think you consider yourself better than they.'
- 'Your mother will:
  - criticize your grammar;
  - misunderstand;
  - think it is foolish.'

What do the judges in your head say?

Key points

- Spontaneity is the heart of creativity.
- Spontaneity is risky.
- Socialization kills spontaneity.
- To increase spontaneity:
  - Do not censor.
  - Be foolish.
  - Be obvious.
  - Celebrate failure.
  - Separate idea generation from evaluation.
  - Recognize the arbitrary nature of judgement.
  - Build the jungle gym.
  - Warm people up.
  - Reiterate the rules of brainstorming.
  - Provide escape hatches.
  - Assess needs.

4

Accepting offers

What would happen if we agreed instead of disagreed? Problems would be solved and there would be more action.

Halpern, Close and Johnson, 1994

The principle

John Lennon met his second wife, Yoko Ono, at a showing of her artwork in New York. He browsed and eventually came upon a magnifying glass that was hanging from the ceiling. Below it, Ono had placed a painter's ladder, and Lennon climbed the ladder, took up the glass and held it to a tiny message written on the ceiling. The single word scribed there was 'Yes'. Lennon said that it was that piece, with that specific word, that kindled his interest in Ono.

The third number-one rule of improv is, 'Say, "Yes, and…".' (The first is 'Make your partner look good.' The second is 'Be spontaneous.') 'Yes, and…' means accept ideas and build on them. 'Yes, and...' is a phrase that is ubiquitous in the improv community. Johnstone discusses the power of 'Yes, and-ing'. 'Yes, & Productions' is the ImprovOlympic producing organization, and www.yesand.com is a major Web site for improvisers. I believe the phrase, as well as the concept, originated with Viola Spolin in her book *Improvisation for the Theater* (1983).

Another way to look at spontaneity, which we discussed in such great detail in the last chapter, is as a willingness to accept what our minds and bodies are offering us. The next step is to accept the 'offers' that come from outside ourselves.

There is a simple exercise, adapted from Johnstone, that improv trainers use to illustrate this concept. 'But vs and' (also called 'Yes, and/Yes, but') is played in two rounds. In the first, five volunteers are asked to plan a company picnic or holiday party. After the first suggestion is made (for example, 'Let's have the party in Hawaii'), each successive idea must begin with the words 'Yes, but...'. It usually goes something like this:

'Let's have the party in Hawaii.'
'Yes, but... that's so far away.'
'Yes, but... we could take a plane.'
'Yes, but... there are so many people.'
'Yes, but... we could have a big roast pig.'
'Yes, but... some people are vegetarian.'
'Yes, but... who cares?'
'Yes, but... your boss is a vegetarian.'
'Yes, but... I'm quitting next week.'

Entertaining, perhaps, but not much of a party plan. If the exercise does not conclude in an argument, it tends to degenerate into lots of discouraged and silent participants staring at each other and the facilitator, devoid of ideas. Everyone is relieved to sit down.

Moving on to round two. Five more volunteers are invited to complete the same task – planning a company party – with one variation. This time, instead of starting their sentences with 'Yes, but...' they begin each offer with the words, 'Yes, *and*...'. With the adjustment, the dialogue progresses in this fashion:

'Let's have the party in Hawaii.'
'Yes, and... let's have a big roast pig.'
'Yes, and... those little tropical drinks with umbrellas.'
'Yes, and... leis.'
'Yes, and... we can charter a jet to take everyone there.'
'Yes, and... we can have fruit and poi for the vegetarians.'
'Yes, and... alcohol!'
'Yes!' (Everyone seems to be for alcohol.)
'Yes, and... we'll get Sam to dance in a grass skirt.'
'Yes!'

This time, the participants report feeling happy, enthusiastic and relaxed. (Even Sam.) Observers agree that this sounds like a much more enjoyable party to attend. Everyone understands that saying 'Yes, but...' is just a cagey way of saying 'No'. Nierenberg and Calero, the authors of *How to Read a Person Like a Book*, say, '"But" is a verbal eraser.' Nothing that comes before it counts. Whereas saying, 'Yes, and...' allows the team members to accept and build on others' offers.

'Offer' is an improv term for anything that can be perceived and accepted. An offer can be verbal, physical, conceptual or emotional. If an actor walks into a scene, fumbles with the door and says, 'Hi, darling, I'm home', the offers inherent in the moment include:

- the words – the fact that she has labelled this place as 'home' and another actor as 'darling';
- the specific tone of voice – is she happy, sad, tired, frustrated, triumphant, casual?
- the objects she may be carrying – does she have bags, an animal, papers, a knife?
- her fumbling with the door;
- the way she walks;
- the way she holds her head.

The number of offers is almost infinite. Any of them can be accepted, ignored or rejected.

In improv, any idea is better than no idea. Since the entire show is being made up on the spot, all that improvisers have is what they and their fellow improvisers agree on at that moment. There is no reality other than the mutually accepted one. As long as someone rejects offers, a scene will stall, and a new idea must be found to jump-start it. Paul Zuckerman, a producer at Chicago City Limits, used to say that refusing to say 'Yes' to an offer is like incessantly driving down the highway and never taking an exit. A scene (or a project) cannot get started until you commit to a destination. Certainly, there may be other towns along the way, but you will never discover the treasures in any of them unless you choose one to visit.

In scripted theatre, the principle is just as important, though a little subtler. The audience 'suspend their disbelief', as the saying goes, in order to accept the reality of the story on the stage. The actors identify, accept and enhance the words of the playwright through their emotional and non-verbal choices. The director and the team design sets, costumes, lighting and movements to highlight the intention of the play and the performances of the cast.

Accepting offers is just as important in non-theatrical settings. Ultimately, saying 'Yes' is the foundation of all relationships. What is flirting but a way of saying, 'Yes, I see you, and I like what I see'? Negotiation is finding the solution that meets all parties' needs – that each side is willing to accept. The sales process consists of getting the customer to say 'Yes' to whatever it is you are selling.

There are subtler rewards for saying 'Yes', too. Team members become sullen, demotivated and uninspired very quickly when their ideas are consistently rejected; whereas, when their ideas are accepted, motivation increases. Individuals begin to feel more competent and a stronger sense of belonging when those around them accept their ideas. Even in the three minutes of participating in the 'But vs and' exercise, in which the stakes are non-existent, participants begin to feel frustrated or invigorated depending on the pattern. Improvisers have labelled the rejection of offers 'blocking', and it is the ultimate taboo in their world. In the world of business, blocking does not hold the same stigma, but the results – resentful and dissatisfied colleagues – may be the same.

Resistance to saying 'Yes'

Most people will accept the concept that saying 'Yes' is valuable. We like our ideas to be accepted, at least to the extent that they receive consideration. Why, then, are we so quick to say 'No'? Here are some common reasons for rejecting offers:

- Saying 'Yes' requires action.
- Someone else might get more credit than we will.
- Someone we don't like is championing an idea.
- Contradicting or debating is a way we have learnt to feel clever.
- The idea offered feels risky/silly/unoriginal (see Chapter 3).
- There is a perceived or actual lack of resources.
- We think the idea is 'bad'.
- We think the idea is impossible to implement.
- We like our own idea better.
- We don't understand the idea.
- We don't recognize that an offer has been made.
- Conflict is exciting.

Keith Johnstone says, 'There are people who prefer to say "Yes", and there are people who prefer to say "No". Those who say "Yes" are rewarded by the adventures they have. Those who say "No" are rewarded by the safety they attain' (1979). Often it may be that simple. Saying 'No' feels safer. Less to do. Less to think about. Less to risk.

Another factor that adds to our penchant for saying 'No' is that it is a well-developed habit. We are simply more experienced at it. A Stanford University business professor, teaching a course on creativity, relates that his students can easily come up with 15 reasons why an idea will not work. That, he says, bespeaks a great deal of intelligence and creativity. Rarely, though, does it enter the students' heads to apply the same talent to generating ideas or devising solutions to potential challenges in the ideas presented. All their business school training has been geared towards finding the problems and seeking out the weak links. Our blocking muscles get much more exercise than our accepting muscles.

Accepting blocks

What is interesting is how easy it is to circumvent blocking. The best improvisers (and most creative problem solvers) are virtually impossible to block successfully, because they see everything as an offer. Alain Rostain, of Creative Advantage, suggests in his idea-generation sessions that participants think about a block or objection to an idea as a springboard for new ideas, rather than as a wall. Once this adjustment is made, a block becomes simply another offer.

My favourite example of an improviser accepting a blatant block and diffusing it happened in a scene about a divorced couple fighting over custody of the children. Early in the scene, Gerri Lawlor, one of Bay Area Theatresports' biggest crowd-pleasers, had pointed a gun at the actor playing her ex-husband and suggested that he hand over their child. The gun was, as is usual in improv, imaginary. (Since improvisers do not know what kind of sets, costumes and objects will be required ahead of time, they become adept at miming or creating 'space objects'.)

When Gerri first put up her fingers, as if holding a gun, the husband lifted his hands, backed away and said 'Take it easy!' The offer of a gun had been made and accepted. Later in the scene, however – perhaps because he thought it would be funny, perhaps because he couldn't think of anything to say – the actor turned to Gerri and said, 'What is that in your hand, anyway? That's not a gun.' Big block. Everyone, on stage and off, held their breath.

Without a pause, Gerri replied, ' It *is* a gun. I put a milk carton over it so that it wouldn't scare the kids.' Gerri accepted the offer inherent in the block (that the gun was unrecognizable), and maintained the reality of the scene. She continued to honour all of the events and assumptions that had come before. She was able to accept her partner's offer by justifying why he might not have thought the gun was a gun. Plus, she justified it in a way that enhanced the scene, by focusing on the mother's relationship with her child, the heart of the scene to begin with. The improvisers present that night analysed and praised her skill. The audience simply cheered.

The power of optimism

Successful collaboration requires Gerri's sort of ebullient optimism. People will say 'No'. Those individuals and teams who believe they can overcome the obstacles will try harder, give up less easily and consequently achieve more. In his book, *Learned Optimism* (1998), Martin Seligman discusses the value of an optimistic outlook. Although studies show that pessimistic individuals may view the world in a more 'realistic' way, optimists tend to succeed more often simply because they expect to. Seligman states that 'organizations, large and small, need optimism; they need people with talent and drive, who are also optimistic. An organization filled with optimistic individuals – or studded with optimistic individuals in crucial niches – has an edge.' Specifically, Seligman suggests that individuals in the following fields need optimistic approaches: 'sales, brokering, presenting and acting, fund-raising, creative jobs, highly competitive jobs, high burnout jobs'. That covers an awful lot of people. The good news, according to Seligman – as you may have divined from the title of his book – is that optimism can be learnt. Improvisers believe so, too, and they take a dual approach to the task.

First of all, improvisers insist on jumping in and accepting ideas regardless of how unrealistic the chance for success seems. Secondly, they do not fear failure. I have found myself introducing new exercises to my students by saying, 'Of course, this is impossible, but let's try it anyway.' The point is that, realistically, we know what we are attempting is bound to fail. (Five people cannot tell the same story at the same time in exactly the same words without planning ahead, for example.) But when we foolishly say 'Yes' to the craziest of ideas, we do, in fact, sometimes succeed.

Speaking in unison

Overview:
- Groups of three to five participants tell a story, answer questions or explain a process in unison, vocally mirroring each other.

Improv topics:
- Spontaneity
- Accepting offers
- Listening and awareness
- Storytelling

Purpose:
- Warm-up
- Energy builder
- Team building
- Creativity
- Communication
- Review

Supplies:
- None

Time:
- 3–5 minutes per group

Number of players:
- 3–5 per group

Game flow:
- Recruit three to five volunteers.
- Give them a title for a story.
- Instruct them to speak in one voice, as if they were one person.
- Ask them a few simple questions to get them warmed up, and then let them proceed to tell the story (eg What is your name? How did you get here today?).
- Coach with questions along the way if necessary.
- Have other groups try it in front of the entire group or play simultaneously.

Variations:
- Have the participants role-play as a guest on a talk show and speak in unison as they answer questions (see 'Experts', page 57).

- Have the participants explain a process or learning point.
- Have two groups of three to five participants have a conversation in unison.

Tips:
- Remind the group that this is a very difficult task. They should expect to make mistakes.
- The trick to successfully speaking in unison is to mirror each other's mouths and 'Yes, and...' the sounds and shapes. You may find that joining a group and helping them along helps.
- Encourage groups to go as fast as they can and still stay together.
- Encourage members of the group to share leadership – both initiating and following.
- If a sentence doesn't make sense, or the group members get out of sync, ask them to repeat what they just said.
- The interviewing versions are easier than the longer narrative versions. Choose a format that the group is comfortable with.

Suggested debrief questions:
- What enables us to complete this task?
- How much did you feel the group shared leadership?
- How much did you initiate?
- How often did you follow?
- When were you most comfortable?
- What does this activity tell us about collaboration?

Source:
- Keith Johnstone, Freestyle Repertory Theatre

Exercising acceptance

Once we decide to accept offers, the muscle is easy to exercise. A 'Yes, and...' story in which players tell a story by adding sentences to a story, each one beginning with the words 'Yes, and...' is one way to do so. Another of my students' favourite 'Yes, and-ing' activities, 'Accept this!' (see page 54), is called 'It's Tuesday' and described in Johnstone's book, *Impro* (1979). In it, one person makes a neutral or 'boring' offer and the person's partner over-accepts that offer. Over-accepting consists of responding as if the offer were incredibly important and then building on it to an outrageous degree. When the second person reaches a conclusion, the first person over-accepts some boring detail of that person's rant and continues. It might go something like this:

Person A: Here's your coffee.
Person B: My coffee! Oh, my coffee. What a glorious elixir! My life's blood. Ah, I cannot live without coffee. I was just about to quit, because I had no energy to go on. But now I can continue. The project will be complete; the company will not go bankrupt. I love coffee! I love *you*! You brought me my coffee and I love you. Can you stay for a while? Have a seat.
Person A: [over-accepting the neutral offer] Have a seat? Have a seat?! I... I don't know what to say. No one has ever asked me to sit down before. I spend all day running around, bringing people coffee. Wow! You want me to sit down? Here? In this chair? This beautifully cushioned, leather chair? Oh, I couldn't. I just... [he begins to weep with joy]...
And so on.

'Accept this!' is a terrific exercise for pointing out the power of emotion. It underlines the fact that accepting offers is as much about having an enthusiastic attitude as it is about the specific response. It is also great practice in saying 'Yes' first and working out why later.

Accept this!

Overview:
- In pairs, participants take turns making neutral, innocuous statements, and over-accepting them.

Improv topics:
- Accepting offers
- Spontaneity

Purpose:
- Warm-up
- Energy builder
- Team building
- Creativity
- Communication

Supplies:
- None

Time:
- 8–15 minutes

Number of players:
- Pairs

Game flow:
- Have the participants get into pairs.
- Pick an A and a B.
- Have the As make some kind of neutral statement (eg 'It's sunny today', 'The report is due on the 17th' or 'You are wearing black shoes').
- Have the Bs respond to the offer with a huge emotion, and rant about the ramifications of the statement. For example, 'I'm wearing black shoes? Oh, no! I thought they were brown. Now my shoes and my trousers won't match. My mother is coming to visit today and when she sees that my shoes and trousers don't match she will humiliate me in front of everyone. I will probably lose my job and eventually be homeless…'
- When B finishes, have him or her make a neutral statement to A, who responds with a different huge emotion and begins a rant.
- The two participants switch back and forth as often as time allows.

Variations:
- Have the second person build from a statement in the first person's rant.
- Provide the neutral statements on slips of paper.
- Provide the emotion with which participants respond.
- Have participants play in groups of four, with the participants responding to each statement in pairs.
- Play in a circle, with participants taking turns directing a statement to someone across the circle who responds.
- Give the participants a process or product and have them rant about the value of it or how it has affected their lives. (This version is a good review activity or idea-generation exercise.)

Tips:
- Encourage the participants to have huge, outrageous responses. They need not be logical.
- Encourage the participants to choose different emotions each time they respond.
- The versions in which participants are playing in pairs at the same time will be less stressful for the participants.
- You may wish to model the activity to increase the participants' willingness to take risks.

Suggested debrief questions:
- What happens when you over-accept?
- How did it feel to express yourself with emotion?
- What emotions were easiest for you to express?
- How did you censor yourself?
- What is the value of accepting and building on offers?
- What does this activity have to do with creativity?

Source:
- Adapted from Keith Johnstone's 'It's Tuesday' exercise

Another simple 'Yes, and-ing' activity is 'Experts'. The familiar format and slightly less hysterical genre make it a preferred choice when working with traditional or slightly reticent corporate clients. A talk show format is set up with a host and a guest. The guest is assigned an area of expertise, and the host interviews him or her. The expert is instructed to feign extreme confidence and answer every question in the affirmative. The interviewer is instructed to respond as if very impressed and to 'Yes, and' the expert's statements by allowing the questions to be inspired by the last answer. The directive to say 'Yes' to all questions produces wild results, and students may resist at first. When coached consistently, though, they submit, and the results are delightful:

> 'So, you've written a book,' the interviewer says.
>
> 'Yes,' the expert responds.
>
> 'I see it's called *Dating Tips for the Shy Giraffe.*' (The group has given the guest the topic of 'animal husbandry', and the performers have begun to talk about 'animal husbands'. From there they have moved to animal dating.)
>
> 'Yes, it is. *Dating Tips for the Shy Giraffe.*'
>
> 'What's tip number 1?'
>
> 'Bring flowers.' (The expert answers quickly, even though he later says he wanted to censor his answer as too obvious.)
>
> 'Flowers, ah, yes, wonderful. And why is it so important for shy giraffes especially to bring flowers?'
>
> 'Well, if there's something there to eat, you don't have to talk.'

The students laugh appreciatively. The expert swears that he did not have any idea where he was going to end up. But by simply saying 'Yes' to his interviewer's questions – and to his own impulses – he created a satisfying and entertaining interchange.

Late in 1999, the California Governor's Council on Y2K Readiness brought in a group of creativity consultants, led by Alain Rostain, to design and facilitate a last-minute idea-generation session. The government officials and business leaders who made up the group wanted to make sure that they had not overlooked any issue. As one of those consultants, I played 'Experts' with the group members. The interviews were set up as if the time were March 2000. The experts played such roles as homemakers, bankers and police officers talking about how the roll-over to the new millennium had affected them. I wish I could say that we discovered some amazing issue that they had overlooked that saved the world. We did not. (Actually, most of the ideas centred on managing PR if nothing happened and the government had to justify spending so much money, so I suppose on some level we were prescient.) The participants did mention, though, that they had had a great time, and planned to use the exercise earlier in the process in the year 9999, when we would have to deal with a similar computer glitch.

Experts

Overview:
- One participant role-plays a subject-matter expert, and the other plays an interviewer. The rest of the participants act as a studio audience, observing and asking questions.

Improv topics:
- Spontaneity
- Accepting offers
- Listening and awareness
- Trust
- Storytelling
- Non-verbal behaviour

Purpose:
- Team building
- Creativity
- Communication
- Needs assessment
- Problem solving
- Review

Supplies:
- Two chairs

Time:
- 7–15 minutes per group

Number of players:
- Pairs

Game flow:
- Ask for two volunteers, one to be the expert, one the interviewer.
- Assign an area of expertise to the expert. (This can be chosen by the facilitator or fielded from the participants.)
- Remind the two players to 'Yes, and…' each other.
- Have the interviewer introduce the guest and interview him or her.
- After a bit, have the audience ask questions.
- Debrief.

Variations:
- Have two or three experts with different attitudes or approaches to the topic.
- Have an expert made up of three participants who answer the questions one word at a time (see 'One-word-at-a-time exercises', page 158).
- Have an expert who speaks gibberish, an interpreter who translates and the interviewer who speaks English (see 'Gibberish press conference', page 146).

Tips:
- For general creativity or communication skills training, pick an outrageous topic (eg fish playing basketball) or a topic that no one in the room knows much about. This diminishes the pressure to get the answers 'right'.
- For visioning and problem solving, use topics that participants are real experts in, and use the format to focus their thinking and tap ideas they may not have thought of.
- Coach the expert to answer 'Yes' to the questions.
- Coach the interviewer to build on the previous answers when asking questions.

Suggested debrief questions:
- What happened when you said 'Yes' as opposed to 'No'?
- What surprised you?
- How did you censor yourself?
- When was this easiest?
- Why was this entertaining?

Source:
- Viola Spolin, the Chicago schools and Theatresports

Drawing it out

'Yes, and-ing' is not only a verbal process. 'Paired drawing' is based on a Johnstone (1979) exercise, 'Eyes'. Participants are asked to draw two dots, which serve as eyes, on a shared piece of paper. Then, in pairs, they draw a face, alternating back and forth, contributing a line or feature each turn. As soon as one of the sketchers hesitates, the drawing is finished. Then two artists, alternating one letter at a time, title it. Charles Schwab employees created the examples in Figures 4.1 to 4.6 as part of a team-building session in San Francisco.

Figure 4.1 Paired drawing: example 1

Figure 4.2 Paired drawing: example 2

Figure 4.3 Paired drawing: example 3

Figure 4.4 Paired drawing: example 4

Figure 4.5 Paired drawing: example 5

Figure 4.6 Paired drawing: example 6

Application

The more power individuals have, the more it matters whether they reject or accept ideas. Managers who kill the suggestions of their staff will soon find they have a staff devoid of ideas or initiative. Trainers who ignore the input of their students will fail to impart their material. Here are some methods for implementing the 'Yes, and...' philosophy.

Assess and strengthen your personal 'Yes, and...' ability

If you wish to encourage certain behaviours, there is no better place to start than with yourself. Start to track your own reactions. How often do you accept others' ideas? When do you say 'No'? Check your analysis with those who report to you. Do they perceive you to be as open as you expected? If you find yourself blocking offers more than you want to, try to work out why. Take a look at the list of reasons people say 'No', as recorded above, and see which ones strike a chord. You might also want to assess the environment in which you work. Do you feel as if your ideas are accepted? If not, how do you react?

   Individuals can do a number of the exercises in this book on their own. Take the time outside the workplace to practise your 'Yes, and-ing' skills. Make up 'Yes, and...' stories. Imagine saying 'Yes' to ideas that you have previously rejected. Pause and reflect on your reasons before saying 'No' to ideas. See if there are ways to use your resistance as a springboard to a solution that builds on the idea. Pledge to say 'Yes' to at least one stupid idea a week.

Capture genius

Andrew Kimball of QBInternational, a consulting firm specializing in human performance with offices in the United States and Europe, tells this story. Consolidated Foods was looking for ideas for new confectionery products. In one of their brainstorming sessions, someone came up with the idea of 'candy that could talk'. The idea was recorded, but rejected by most people as ridiculous and impractical. It wasn't as if you could get tape recorders that small, even if people would be willing to swallow them. An executive in the group, however, was taken with the concept and pursued it. Upon further investigation, he found out that his chemists had been working on a process for encasing carbon dioxide in a sugar shell. When placed in water these small pellets would explode, making crackling and popping sounds. In other words, they talked. The CEO devoted lots of resources to the project, and 'Pop Rocks', which had one of the most successful new confectionery debuts in history, was born.

It is not enough to generate original ideas. Those ideas must be nurtured and brought to fruition. The Innovation Network, an international community devoted to the study of innovation, says that formal idea-generation sessions yield only 20 per cent of organizations' innovative ideas leading to products. That is not so bad, really, considering that much less than 20 per cent of people's time is spent in those sessions. However, it does suggest that we should be on the lookout for breakthrough ideas at all times. And remember, it is not the ideas that seem practical and safe that need a champion.

Enhance teamwork

If I were able to teach a team only one principle to make it more effective, I would choose 'Yes, and-ing'. Teams that accept and build on each other's ideas are more creative and more collaborative, and have less conflict. The 'Yes, and-ing' exercises in this book will enable teams to practise supporting each other, maximize their creative output and build trust.

Team-building workshops are increasingly popular. The next time you wish to enhance teamwork, whether it is in the context of a workshop or in the course of daily interaction, use a 'Yes, and-ing' exercise.

Motivate

Again, the elements of motivation are perceived needs for competence, autonomy and relatedness (Richter, 2001). Accepting and building on individuals' ideas are great ways to motivate people on all three levels. Learners will feel more competent if the trainer acknowledges and builds on the skills they already possess. When employees have their ideas accepted, they feel both a sense of control over their environments and a sense of affiliation with those who accept them. In general, team members who feel their experience and input are valued will be more engaged and happier.

Key points

- Say 'Yes, and…': accept offers and add to them.
- Spontaneity is a way of saying 'Yes' to yourself.
- 'But' is a verbal eraser.

- An 'offer' can be anything.
- Saying 'Yes' is the bedrock of all relationships.
- We can come up with all sorts of reasons to say 'No'.
- Saying 'No' (blocking) is a well-developed habit.
- Blocking can be overcome.
- Optimism is the willingness to overcome obstacles and continue to say 'Yes'.
- Assess and strengthen your own ability.
- Capture genius.
- Enhance teamwork.
- Motivate through acceptance.

5

Listening and awareness

Imagining should be as effortless as perceiving.

Keith Johnstone (1979)

The principle

Close your eyes. All right, open them or you will not be able to read. But do not look. Is there a phone in the room? (If not, pick a phone with which you are familiar.) What colour is the body of the phone? What shape is the receiver? Is there a display? Is it backlit? Are the numbers on the handset or the base? How many other buttons are there on the phone? Any writing? Who manufactured the phone? OK. Take a look. How did you do?

Before an offer can be accepted, it must be recognized – not as easy a task as one might think. There is so much information bombarding us at any given moment that to make sense of it we blot out and distort the data. We make choices about what to focus on. Who has time to study the phone on their desk? Why bother? And yet, what important information do we miss – by not listening to instructions, not hearing feedback, not recognizing discrepancies between what we believe and what exists?

Dr Francis Crick, one of the two scientists who mapped the structure of DNA, went on to study the brain. He has been quoted as saying, '80 per cent of what we experience as true, we make up.' Even if the statement is only 20 per cent true, it leaves us plenty of room to doubt ourselves.

Some of us played a game when we were children called 'telephone'. Remember? You would whisper a phrase into someone's ear and they would whisper it to someone else and so on until it came out in some mangled version at the other end. Although many of us have played that game or a similar one, we still expect to receive and pass on messages without significant distortion. Shouldn't we know better?

Enhancing listening

For those who do wish to enhance their listening skills, there are relatively simple techniques. They include asking questions, checking understanding by feeding back information, and taking notes. As improvisers, though, we do not get the chance to double-check our assumptions or write down details. The skill that improvisers work on developing is the ability to acquire and interpret a high volume of information the first time around.

'Story exchange' serves as a workout for listening muscles, and as a jolt, highlighting the complexity of listening well. Participants pair off and take turns telling a short story from their lives. Then they switch partners and tell the story that they have just heard as if it were their own, trying to repeat the words, gestures and inflections of the story as accurately as possible. Again the participants switch partners, telling the story that they heard most recently. Finally, the entire group comes together and each participant recounts the last story told to him or her. At the end of this process, not one of the stories is completely accurate. Some are so different as to be unrecognizable.

'Story exchange' reminds us of the frailty of our communication skills. However, our ability to receive complete and accurate information can be enhanced through practice. Improvisers who practise listening visibly (no pun intended) improve their skills. Chris Oyen, one of my first improv coaches, amazed me one night when I was baby-sitting his two-month-old daughter. Rebecca was a beautiful but colicky baby, and she was screaming. There was a baseball game on TV. The dog was snoring, and Chris was passionately discussing an event that had happened at the theatre the night before. After about half an hour of this mayhem, Chris's friend came in from the kitchen and asked me, 'What's the score?' I had no idea. It had been at least 20 minutes since any of us had paid attention to baseball, as far as I could tell. Chris, however, interrupted himself in mid-sentence, turned to his friend and said, 'It's 7–3 Mets, bottom of the sixth, men on first and third, two outs.' Perhaps I should not have been surprised. Much of Chris's brilliance on stage came from his capacity for hyper-awareness. He is a director at Disney World now, and I'm sure his superpower helps him in that role, as well.

Story exchange

Overview:
- Participants exchange short stories from their lives. After exchanging stories, they cycle through a number of rounds in which they tell the stories they have just heard as if they were their own. Finally, the group comes together in a circle, and each member again tells the last story they have heard. Think a giant, complex game of telephone.

Improv topics:
- Listening and awareness
- Storytelling
- Trust
- Accepting offers
- Non-verbal behaviour

Purpose:
- Ice-breaker
- Team building
- Creativity
- Communication

Supplies:
- 3 × 5 cards
- Pens

Time:
- 25–50 minutes

Number of players:
- 10–20

Game flow:
- Pass out 3 × 5 cards and pens.
- Assign participants a number and have them write it on their card, as big and as legibly as possible.
- Have the participants find a partner and decide who will be an A and who will be a B.
- Have the As tell the Bs a story from their life. The stories should be:
  - true;
  - about 60–90 seconds long;

- from any period or aspect of their lives (eg something that happened this week, something that happened in childhood).
- The Bs should *listen only*. They should not interrupt or ask questions.
- When the As finish, have the Bs tell a story
- Have the partners exchange 3 × 5 cards. Everyone now has the card with the number of the story they just heard.
- Ask everyone to find a new partner.
- Each person now tells the story that he or she has just heard, in the first person (*'I* took the goldfish…') as accurately as possible, as if it is his or her story. Stress that participants are to attempt to tell the story exactly as they heard it. (Note: Hold off telling the participants that they will have to repeat their partner's story until this point.)
- When both participants have told their stories, ask them to exchange 3 × 5 cards and find a new partner.
- This time, ask people to make sure that they are not paired with someone who has a card with a number they have already seen. This process ensures that people will not get their own story back or hear the same story more than once.
- Again, have the participants exchange stories (as above) and swap cards.
- Have the participants form a circle, and one by one tell the stories that they have just heard.

Variations:
- Assign a specific topic for the stories (eg a story involving technology, a story from childhood, a management experience).
- Demo version (this version is good for use with large groups, when having each person tell a story would be unwieldy, and also useful for allowing participants to view the process of the stories changing and track how the changes occur):
  - Ask for 4 volunteers (A, B, C and D).
  - Send C and D out of the room.
  - Have A tell a story to B.
  - Then C re-enters and B tells the story he or she has just heard from A.
  - Then D re-enters and C tells D A's story as told by B.
  - Finally, D retells A's story to the group at large.
  - Debrief.

Tips:
- Refrain from discussion of the changes in the stories until everyone has shared.
- Let the individuals volunteer to go next, rather than going in order around the circle. This will help to keep the entire group engaged.

Suggested debrief questions:
- How did we do?
- Did anyone not recognize his or her story?
- What kinds of changes were there in your stories?
- What sorts of things can you listen for (facts, feelings, intentions)?
- What was your experience of listening to the stories?
- How did your experience change when you knew you would have to repeat the story you were hearing?
- How can we become more skilled listeners?

Source:
- Adapted from Viola Spolin and Theatresports

Increasing awareness

We pick up information both consciously and unconsciously. Increasing listening and awareness skills is less about sensing more things, and more about sensing things more consciously. At any given moment there are events and facts that we are paying attention to, and a whole host of other details that are in our broader, less conscious awareness. What the best improvisers are able to do is widen their circle of consciousness to include more information.

The West Coast improviser Stephen Kearin has amazed audiences from California to Finland with his attention to the smallest detail. Once Kearin was teaching a class on making sound effects with one's voice. (This is a common technique in improv performances, and Kearin is one of the masters of it.) The students were practising making the sound of a chain-saw. In one scene, a student, lying on the floor, pretended to saw off his leg. He attempted a chainsaw sound, and Stephen stopped him.

'All right,' he said, 'your sound is generally OK, but what are you cutting?'

The student replied, 'Uh… my leg.'

'Yeah, all right, but listen,' Stephen continued. He then performed his version of the sound, changing it subtly three or four times as he drew the imaginary blade through his limb. 'Did you hear it as it cut through?' he said, 'Not just "leg". Flesh, bone, flesh, floor.'

The lesson of Stephen's admittedly gory demonstration was that it is not the dexterity of an improviser's mouth, but the specificity of his awareness that elevates him to greatness.

Think back to the exercise at the beginning of the chapter. How many times have you picked up that phone I asked you to describe? You do not need any special talent to know what it looks like. All you need to do is to consciously focus your attention on it. Under hypnosis, you would be able to describe the phone more exactly. US police forces have used hypnosis when interviewing crime victims about the details of their assailants and the circumstances of the crime, because they know that we perceive much more detail than we have available to us in our conscious awareness.

Facts, feelings, intentions

Developing our awareness consists not only of increasing our capacity for information, but in heightening our awareness of the different types of information that can be gleaned. In the 'Story exchange' exercise, a few different types of mistakes occur when participants retell the stories. The most straightforward errors are factual ones. A name, a number or a place gets changed or left out. The second type involves emotion or attitude. Whereas the first storyteller might feel excited and positive, the person repeating the story might express confusion or apathy. Finally, participants misconstrue the intent of the stories they hear. In other words, there are three things that we can listen for when we listen:

- facts;
- feelings;
- intentions.

Facts are the simplest to perceive. They are objective and concrete – not that we always get them right by any means. Some actors must work hard to remember their lines. Improvisers notoriously struggle to remember the character names they have given each other. Some improv companies have gone so far as to implement a rule that makes everyone go by their real name on stage. Still, although we may fail to remember these details, they are ultimately black and white, right or wrong, easy to track. Improving our ability to perceive and retain facts simply entails strengthening our focus and memory.

Perceiving feelings is a little trickier. Especially in business settings, we are taught to hide and ignore our feelings. We are not used to focusing on emotions, except in the safest and most intimate environments. However, the feelings of the communicator may be more important that the specific facts. Here is an example of how the emotional content of a story got missed during 'Story exchange'.

Stacey, a woman in her late 20s, described how, as a first-year student at her university, she and her room-mate had heard a spot on the radio advertising fur coats for '$39.99'. They gleefully headed to the store to pick out their coats, expecting a small, seedy storefront – but then, they were students: seediness was part of the fun. When they arrived, the store was luxurious. Rows and rows of beautiful minks and foxes, sables and chinchilla hung on racks of brass. Saleswomen waited on the girls like royal servants, and when Stacey and her friend had picked out their coats, the saleswomen offered them wine in celebration, asking 'Will that be cash or charge?'

The girls decided they could pay cash – even with tax the bill couldn't come to more than $50. They said so, pulling out their money. The saleswomen went pale. 'Ahem. No,' they said, 'the coats are three *thousand*, nine hundred and ninety-nine dollars. Not $39. These are *real* fur coats, you know.' And so the girls left without their garments.

In the original telling, Stacey expressed deep embarrassment. Later, she confirmed that she remembered this incident as one of the most humiliating of her life. By the time the story got to the fourth storyteller, though, it was a story of teenage mischief: 'two hip young college chicks set out to torture the evil fur-hocking sales ladies'. The thing was, most of the factual details stayed the same. It was the tone of the voice, the emphasis and the look in the teller's eye that changed. (It is the ability to recognize and communicate these subtle differences, by the way, that separates the great actors from the rest.)

Sometimes, the details of a story are just conduits for expressing emotional content. How many of us have said things like, 'You always interrupt me,' or 'Why don't you ever include me in meetings?' Just as many of us have had someone respond to us by saying, 'I don't *always* interrupt you.' In these cases, it is the feeling not the detail that it is important to hear. Unless the emotional content is addressed, all the data in the world will not result in clear communication. That is not to say that data are unimportant. If you are building a rocket ship, the specific numbers matter. In most of our communications, though, facts are just one aspect of the message. And imagine how much more complex the communication becomes when it is cross-cultural.

This brings us to the third kind of information we can listen for: the intention of the communication. Understanding the point of a message qualifies as the most important aspect of listening. To put it in terms of our discussions so far, at any given moment we are accepting a huge number of offers and ignoring others. A good listener's job is twofold: to expand the amount of information that he or she can take in, and then quickly to assess the relative value of that information. In order to understand the point of a story, we need to be able to evaluate what data are crucial and what are peripheral.

At Freestyle Rep, I had a colleague – we'll call her Kelly – who was infamous for missing the most valuable pieces of information, while accepting some other innocuous offer. I remember a scene in which she played an old dowager. Her partner entered the scene as her butler. He was carrying a tray and, as he spoke, he set the dishes and pot on the table in front of her.

'Madam,' he said, 'I must inform you that your son has just returned from the war. He is alive, although it looks as though he is missing a number of limbs.'

'Ooh,' Kelly cooed in response, 'Tea! Yummy.'

The actor playing the butler accepted this offer as an indication that Kelly's character was a little batty. (Remember, it is impossible to be blocked.) But the fact that it was teatime certainly was not the richest offer put forth in the scene.

Harvesting inspiration

In *Jump Start Your Brain* (1996), a popular book on corporate innovation, Doug Hall suggests that, although we often think of the act of creation as a magical, internal process, in fact our minds work more like manufacturing factories. We put raw material in, play with it, restructure, modify, add to it and then have a product come out the other end. The best way to create is to stimulate your imagination from the outside by dumping as much external content into your brain as possible, and letting it serve as the raw stuff from which ideas are formed – rather like feeding threads into a loom or car parts on to an assembly line. Barbara Scott, of Bay Area Theatresports, is heralded by her fellow improvisers for her ability to receive and understand their offers. Barbara says that she has become skilled at this because she cannot come up with ideas of her own. She is being modest, but the resulting principle is valuable. Enhancing our listening and awareness abilities can increase not only communication but also creativity. Here are some non-game-based activities that you can try to enhance awareness:

- Eavesdrop on conversations.
- Mimic personalities on TV.
- Pay attention to the details of habitual activities (eg brushing your teeth, washing dishes, petting the dog).
- Close your eyes and quiz yourself on the details of the room you are in, your partner's clothing, your kitchen sink.
- Watch strangers and make up stories about what their lives are like, based on behaviours you observe.
- When someone tells you a story, feed back your interpretation of his or her point.

To improve their abilities to perceive facts, feelings and intentions, actors practise 'being in the moment', which means heightening one's awareness of what is happening right now. With all of our inner voices, and external pressures, being in the moment requires great discipline.

The listening curve

Here is the other side of the story. QBInternational teaches a model, designed by Ralph Nichols, that suggests people's ability to listen over time maps something like the curve shown in Figure 5.1.

People are able to pay attention for a given amount of time, but then some word or other concern captures their attention and they drift off. When they refocus, a gap exists in what they have heard so they are listening at a lower level of efficiency.

There are two facts that make this reality especially discouraging. First, the amount of time that studies have shown people can concentrate is about 90 seconds. (And that was in 1964. These days, advertisers believe the time-

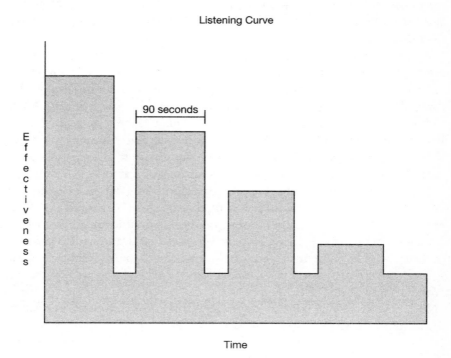

Figure 5.1 The listening curve

frame is more like 6–8 seconds.) Second, the cleverer that listeners are, the more quickly their listening degenerates, since more intelligent people tend to make faster and more frequent connections, and therefore have their minds spin off at a tangent more easily. If this is the case, how can we ever communicate effectively?

Facilitating listening and awareness

Actors who must play the same role eight times a week for months know that concentration unfailingly lags. Performers report whole evenings that they cannot remember – rather like driving a familiar route and finding yourself at your doorstep without remembering the journey. Whereas actors have a planned route, most of us do not. These lapses can have dire consequences. Improvisers know that their partner will be distracted sometimes. For goodness sake, there are scores of people staring at them and an imaginary environment to keep track of. Therefore, in addition to practising awareness skills, improvisers practise communicating clearly so that the information they are relating will be easier to receive. They train themselves to repeat information – like a character's name – over and over. They also learn to state their intentions clearly so that their partner does not have to struggle to discern them.

When students begin improvising, they resist explicitly voicing their intentions. The practice seems unnatural or too obvious. The most experienced improvisers, on the other hand, articulate their feelings and intentions blatantly. Strangely enough, audiences never seem to mind. Or even notice. An improviser will say, 'Happy Birthday. Here's a present for you. It's a puppy', and the audience will be astonished when another improviser thinks to jump out of the box – an imaginary one, remember – as a puppy. 'Oh, that was so creative,' they will say of the second actor.

I was sold on the power of blatantly articulating intentions on stage, when I was picked as a volunteer during the show, *Fool Moon*. The performers in the show, David Shiner of Cirque du Soleil fame and Bill Irwin, are brilliant clowns, who perform an involved first-date scene with an audience member – in this case, me. Neither of them speaks in the show, but while I was on stage they were talking to me the entire time. 'How are you feeling?' 'You're doing great!' 'OK, look over there.' 'When I ask you to kiss me, say "No".' Each step of the way they coached me, in voices easy to hear and understand. Here's the amazing part. No one noticed! Not even my date. In the intermission, everyone came up to me, convinced that I must have been a plant. How could I have known what to do? How could I have supported them so well?

In a way, the audience members were right. I was not acting naturally, following my own impulses and making my own choices. But I had not been briefed ahead of time. I was briefed on stage, at the moment, in front of everyone. When I told my date that Irwin and Shiner had been speaking to me, he was shocked. He had not seen or heard a thing.

A technique I learnt at Creative Advantage has helped me use the power of straightforward communication in proposals for potential customers. Before presenting my design ideas, I include a section called 'Our understanding', which summarizes the clients' needs and objectives. When I first began writing proposals, I interpreted the clients' concerns in my own words. I had to sound intelligent, right? I could not just parrot what they had told me. Now, I do exactly that. I repeat their words as exactly as I can. And the clients love it. I have had at least half a dozen of them tell me that it was my insightful analysis of their needs that convinced them.

The mysterious something else

There is a final piece to this puzzle. No matter how much time we spend dissecting and heightening awareness, there is an unidentifiable component to it. Del Close and Charna Halpern talk about the concept of a 'group mind', saying:

> People who have never experienced it may be sceptical, dismissing it as New Age nonsense, but the group mind is a very real phenomenon. This is not to say that each person can read the others' minds or project specific thoughts; but when a group mind is achieved, its members have a very strong sense of the group as an entity of its own, and connect with its feelings and requirements.

(Halpern, Close and Johnson, 1994)

'Group counting' illustrates this intangible connection that individuals can form with one another. The group stands in a circle and focuses on a spot or object in the centre of the floor. The goal is to count 'one, two, three...' and so on, with each successive number supplied by one and only one of the group members. The trick is that there is no order in which the participants say a number, and no patterns or signals allowed. Each member of the group is required to feel when it is his or her turn to contribute a number. If more than one person offers a number at the same time, the group begins again from 'one'.

'Group counting' comes as close to magic as any of the exercises I know. When I first discovered it, I thought, 'Well, sure, the odds say that if they try long enough, eventually people should be able to count to 20. What's the big deal?' Very quickly, though, I realized that the activity could not be explained away that easily. My students counted to higher and higher numbers each week. By the end of a six-week session, it was not unusual to have groups counting to 70, 80, 100 on the first or second try. That's not statistics.

For all its mystery, I have used 'Group counting' successfully with participants as seriously business-oriented as European corporate executives. There are straightforward lessons that groups learn through this exercise – things like if there are 15 people in a group, and you are counting to 20, each person, on average, gets to say only one or two numbers. If you have 22 people, two of them, at least, must remain silent. And those people who do refrain from saying a number will contribute just as much to the achievement of the goal as those who speak. Still, the lesson with most impact remains for me the power of our instinctual awareness of others, and how quickly we can develop and harness it.

Group counting

Overview:
- The members of the group count from 1 to 20 without deciding which participant will say the next number. There is no established pattern of who speaks next or tacit, conscious communication about order. Anyone may say the next number. If two or more people say a number at the same time, however, the group begins again at 1.

Improv topics:
- Listening and awareness
- Trust

Purpose:
- Team building
- Communication
- Closing

Supplies:
- None

Time:
- 3–10 minutes

Number of players:
- 4–20

Game flow:
- Have the participants stand in a circle.
- Explain that the group will count from 1 to 20, in order, all whole numbers, no tricks.
- Have them close their eyes or focus on the centre of the circle (you may wish to place an object in the centre to facilitate focus).
- Each person can say a number whenever they wish, with the exception that they cannot say two numbers in a row.
- There is no established pattern or secret communication (eg no eye contact, no skipping every other person in the circle).
- Finally, and most importantly, whenever two or more people start to say a number at the same time, the group begins again at 1.

Variations:
- Count to 10 or 15.
- Continue to count until a mistake is made.
- Recite the alphabet one letter at a time.
- Tell a word-at-a-time story beginning with 'Once' 'upon' 'a' 'time', in which you start at the beginning of a new story each time more than one person says a word. (Note: This is a very advanced exercise and should only be tried after a group has become very good at counting.)

Tips:
- This exercise is the best I know for highlighting the idea that good teamwork depends on some ephemeral quality that it is hard to identify. If you run this exercise on an ongoing basis, a group will quickly improve – counting to 60, 80, 100.
- Remind the group that there is not some secret trick. Counting to 20 one person at a time would be easy if you planned who went next. What's the fun in that?
- The secret to success is also not speed. If they are having a hard time, remind the participants to breathe and take their time.
- If there is a group of 15, and you are counting to 20, on average each member will get to say one to two numbers. That means if someone says three numbers, someone else must say none in order for the group to succeed. Remind the members of this if they are struggling.
- You may wish to coach the participants to 'say a number when it is your turn – whatever that means to you'. This phrase highlights the instinctual nature of the activity.
- Allow the group to fail. If they feel frustrated, you can coach them to pause and do the above.
- This is a great way to end a session. You may wish to let the exercise speak for itself without extensive debriefing.

Suggested debrief questions:
- How did that feel?
- When did you choose to say a number?
- When did you choose to say silent?
- How did people contribute to success?
- Why do you think we're getting better at this? (after a number of sessions)
- How is this like group processes at work?

Source:
- Bay Area Theatresports, adapted from a Zen meditation practice

Application

As a trainer, it does not matter how much you know if you cannot communicate with your students. And managers who are unable to gather and interpret information from their employees will find themselves at a significant disadvantage. The following sections indicate some areas on which to focus.

Enhance your own skills

All of the activities suggested in this chapter are recommended for trainers or managers, as well as for their groups. Trainers must be able to assess what their students understand, how they are feeling and what confusions they are trying to express. Just like performing, training requires people to take in a large amount of information, even as they are presenting. In order to be successful, trainers must have highly honed awareness skills.

I knew a trainer who had a brilliant mind and, in theory, designed terrific courses. In practice, he often lost his students because he got so involved in presenting his material that he failed to notice when they were tired or perplexed. Participants would shift in their chairs, whisper to each other or fall asleep, and Joe would continue. At that point, he may as well have been presenting to stuffed dummies for all the learning that was happening.

Similarly, a manager whom I worked with would consistently answer a different question from the one she had been asked. She was so sure of her answers that she anticipated the question without taking time to absorb the heart of it. Questions are little flags that signal unmet needs. If we cannot effectively hear and understand them, we will miss opportunities to satisfy them.

Read between the lines

Not all communication will be straightforward. Sometimes individuals will hide information intentionally. Other times they themselves may be unaware of their real message. Do not be satisfied with a cursory understanding of what people tell you. Look for discontinuities between the words they use and the feelings they express non-verbally. Search for the reason that someone has taken an action or made a statement. If students ask you to repeat something, they may not have heard you, they may not understand the principle or they may disagree. If the impetus for asking was either of the last reasons, merely repeating your statement will not help.

Often you will find clues in the way the question is asked or the answer is received that will let you know if you have provided a solution.

By the way, this attitude can be useful in real life, too. A friend of mine was in a relationship that ended, she said, when she and her boyfriend started taking what the other said at face value. They both ended up feeling misunderstood and uncared about.

Train the team

Because we have been listening since the day we were born (if not before), we do not think of listening as a skill that needs to be learnt. The simple act of discussing the pitfalls and techniques of listening can improve a team's effectiveness. By also engaging in listening activities, teams can not only augment their listening skills but also learn more about each other. As therapists know, tenacious conflicts can disappear as soon as individuals feel they have been heard.

Listening exercises also serve as warm-up activities. Before asking people to take in new information, remind them what skills doing so entails.

Check for understanding

No matter how vigilantly we try to pay attention, we will misunderstand. There is just too much information coming through too many of our own filters for us to receive messages 100 per cent accurately. Remember Dr Crick's quote? '80 per cent of what we perceive to be true, we make up.' The remedy is simple. Check your understanding.

As a consultant at QBInternational, one of the courses I deliver is sales training. A staple technique taught in the course is to ask questions and then to confirm understanding. We have found these simple skills aid communication in the United States, in France, in Japan, wherever we travel. When I teach the class, I try to model the behaviour, confirming understanding of what my students are saying, even when I am sure it is not necessary. I am relatively sure I am at least an above-average listener, but to my chagrin I often find that there are pieces of information I have missed or misinterpreted. I will say it again. Check for understanding.

Separate observable behaviours from interpretations

As coaches, we need to be adept at assessing performance and giving feedback. As we do, we must remember that objective reality is not the same as our interpretations. Listening for intentions and reading between the lines are useful, as we have said. However, remember to distinguish interpretation from the objective observable behaviours that led to them. And when you speak to someone you are coaching, make sure you ground your assumptions in those behaviours. The individual being coached is likelier to accept and benefit from feedback when it is articulated this way.

Let's take the example of Gail (not her real name), a manager whom a colleague of mine, let's call her Susan, was coaching. The manager struck Susan as arrogant and rather petulant. That was her interpretation. Gail's actual behaviours were rolling her eyes when Susan offered suggestions and telling Susan that her ideas would never work. Gail told stories about how lazy and belligerent her workers were, and that, if it were not for her hard work, nothing would ever get done. Rather than beginning with her own assumptions, Susan began by listing Gail's actions – concrete behaviours that Susan had seen and heard. Then Susan asked Gail to explain her intentions and interpretations of those behaviours. As it turned out, Gail had replaced a very popular manager and felt that her staff did not like her. Her intention was to save face in the face of antagonistic co-workers. After their conversation, Susan was better able to address Gail's problems, and Gail was more willing to listen.

Articulate your intentions

Just as we make assumptions about others, they make assumptions about us. And the more authority people have, the less likely they are to know what conclusions others are reaching. When someone has power over us, we scrutinize the smallest behaviours for clues to that person's thoughts and feelings. In order to avoid incorrect and potentially damaging attributions, err on the side of articulating why you are doing whatever you do. Explain how you reached decisions. Share the thoughts behind particular activities and instructional designs. Frame your questions so that people do not feel attacked. It is unrealistic to expect that others will understand us all the time. The more straightforward and complete your communication, the more effective and pleasant your interactions will be.

Feed creativity

As we become more aware, we will find our creativity increasingly stimulated. Continue to provide sensory input to trigger creative thinking through quotes, physical objects, music, colours and stories. Our heightened senses can provide us with internal massages. Awareness is not just hard work; it is also glorious fun.

Key points

- Before an offer can be accepted it must be recognized.
- Listening is more complex that we think.
- There are three types of information to listen and watch for: facts, feelings and intentions.
- Enhancing awareness entails making more of our unconscious processes conscious.
- Once information is received it must be analysed and prioritized.
- Receiving information stimulates creativity.
- Enhance awareness through practice.
- Make it easier for others to listen to you by articulating your desires blatantly.
- Enhance your skills.
- Read between the lines.
- Train the team.
- Check for understanding.
- Separate observable behaviours from interpretations.
- Articulate your intentions.
- Feed creativity.

6

Storytelling

Our knowledge of the world is more or less equivalent to the set of experiences that we have had, but our communication is limited by the number of stories we know to tell… Storytelling and understanding are functionally the same thing.

Roger C Schank (1990)

God made man, because he loves stories.

Elie Wiesel (1966)

The principle

A couple of years ago, a gaggle of QBInternational consultants found themselves in Paris, delivering a sales course for over a hundred participants from all over Europe. As the participants went off to prepare for their afternoon role-plays, the trainers, a diverse group ourselves, from Scotland to India, gathered in the back of the room, and somehow a discussion of storytelling techniques began. We shared various storytelling activities, and moved on to an increasingly enthusiastic exploration of their use in training situations. Our ideas for application ranged from capturing participants' attention to assessing needs to increasing retention to enhancing teamwork to reducing conflict and solving problems. By the time our training participants were ready, we had decided that story was the foundation of all learning, and the seeds for StoryNet LLC, my personal consulting company, had been sown.

We were incredibly proud of ourselves, too. What geniuses we were to realize the profound value of storytelling. Of course, we were neither alone nor ground-breaking in our appreciation. Storytelling is an age-old method of teaching. From the bonfire gatherings of cave dwellers through to modern times, in virtually all societies, stories have formed the foundation of historical and cultural awareness. And storytelling has recently become a widely popular focus in the corporate world in the United States. In 2000, the American Society for Training and Development devoted an issue of their publication, *Info-line*, to storytelling. Dozens of books, including *Tell Me a Story* by Roger C Schank (1990), *Tales for Trainers* by Margaret Parkin (1998) and *Managing by Storying Around* by David Armstrong (1992), advocate the immense value of stories to aid communication and learning. Parkin quotes two studies that have shown the pedagogical power of narrative, finding that students who were told stories made fewer conceptual and technical errors, applied concepts to more varied situations and had an better overall grasp of the content than those students who were given lectures devoid of narrative.

When we are told a story, we engage much more of ourselves than we do when we are presented with mere facts. Our emotions are triggered, associations are stimulated and memories are activated. That is why politicians have such success with anecdotes. The person with the good story beats the person with the accurate facts more often than not.

I heard an interview on radio recently with the new head of the radio station's news services department. He said that, when he had first taken the job, it had been his intention to do away with the reporting of poll results. He felt the news staff depended on polls too much, especially since he was not convinced that polls were all that reliable, informative or compelling in the first place. He was forced to give up his plan, though, because he met with such distress when he suggested it.

'But what will we report?' his staff said.

'What about going out and interviewing people?' he suggested.

'But that's just anecdotal evidence,' they objected.

'Funny,' he said. 'We used to call it the news.'

There is a reason we speak of news *stories*. Poll numbers may be easier to acquire, and have the ring of more objective truth, but they are neither more trustworthy nor more interesting data. People learn more from stories and like them better than dry statistics or procedures.

David Armstrong, the vice-president of Armstrong International, believed so strongly in the power of storytelling as a management tool that he incorporated it into every aspect of his family's business, and eventually completely replaced the policy manual with stories. In the foreword to Armstrong's book, *Managing by Storying Around* (1992), Tom Peters says, 'The wild and woolly marketplace is demanding that we burn the policy manuals and knock off the incessant memo writing; there's just no time for it. It's also demanding that we empower people – everyone – to constantly take initiatives. And it turns out that stories are a – if not *the* – leadership answer to both issues.'

The heart of theatre

Storytelling is also the heart of theatre. Theatre's power lies in its ability to tell compelling, moving, exciting, entertaining, cathartic stories. Audiences get to love, fight, grow old, die and sing through the characters they watch. Religious movements gave birth to theatrical events, and great art has blossomed to carry its message. The theatre has often been censored in times of political unrest, since governments recognized its power to move hearts and influence public opinion. Nothing is as powerful as a good story.

Improvisers develop all the skills that we have discussed so far in order to create thrilling narratives. When an improviser is spontaneous, and recognizes, accepts and builds on offers, stories will naturally result. Human beings are storytellers. Storytelling is such an organic process, Johnstone says, 'It must be obvious that when someone insists that they "can't think up a story", they really mean that they "won't think up a story"' (1979).

Given the ancient, organic and pervasive nature of storytelling in our lives, much of the training in storytelling comes down to making the unconscious processes that we already employ conscious. Since improvisers create narratives collaboratively and without the benefit of revision, they have become especially attuned to skills needed to build satisfying stories. Their exercises and philosophies can inform both individual storytelling skills and collaborative learning environments.

To tell a story, we make choices about which connections to highlight, which paths to follow and which details to focus on. In scripted theatre, it is the playwright who wrestles with the structure of the story first, later turning to the director and actors for input. In improvised theatre, the process begins and ends with collaboration. Various improv companies have discovered alternative approaches to creating stories collaboratively, based on temperament, stylistic preference and simple trial and error. The following sections give some of the basic concepts and tools that have helped my students and clients.

Reincorporation

At the most basic level, the quality that differentiates a story from a mere sequence of unrelated events is meaningful connection. A simple way to achieve that connection is to reincorporate. Reincorporating means that you bring back later whatever it is you introduced in the beginning. The next time you go to a film, pay close attention to the first 20 minutes or so. Make note of the cutaway shots – the shots, not of people, but of objects or scenery. The chances are that if there is a cutaway shot of an object that seems unrelated to the action of that moment, the object may be important later on.

Recently, a friend and I went to see *What Lies Beneath*, a supernatural thriller staring Michelle Pfeiffer and Harrison Ford. At one point early on, the two of them are driving across a country bridge, on the way to a party. Ford's character decides to check his messages, or some such innocuous thing, on his mobile phone. He cannot get through, and Pfeiffer says, 'Oh, you can't get a signal while you are on the bridge.' My friend immediately turned to me and said, 'Someone's going to be trying to call for help while crossing this bridge.' Sure enough, 90 minutes later, Pfeiffer was screaming into a dead phone, racing for the other side of the river.

Film makers, of course, know how the film will end, and can plant foreshadowing events. Improvisers, since they do not know how the scene will end, need to make whatever they set up at the beginning important after the fact. Reincorporating is foreshadowing in reverse. From the audience, the results look like magic. 'How did they know to do that thing with the mobile phone?' an improv audience will think. The principle of storytelling is the same whether writing or improvising. Whatever you set up in the beginning, you had better bring back at the end. As playwright Anton Chekhov put it, 'If you pull out a gun in Act I, it had better go off in Act III.'

Patterns

The practice of reincorporating is surprisingly satisfying. Del Close builds on the concept by talking about the 'game' of the scene (Halpern, Close and Johnson, 1994). This technique is another way of recognizing connections and continuing to reincorporate past events. Any of you who have children will know that patterns can be captivating. A child will play peek-a-boo for hours.

A strong crowd-pleasing scene of the past few years at Bay Area Theatresports had a very clear 'game' or pattern at its heart. The scene began with an improviser lying on the floor and saying to two others, 'Now, kids, no more practical jokes.' The rest of the scene became a series of increasingly outrageous practical jokes played by the kids on the father, culminating in the explosion of the family dog. The audience went wilder with each successive repetition of the pattern. The pattern went like this:

The father says, 'Ahh, ow! Grr. Don't do that again, kids.'
The children say, 'Yes, Daddy, sorry.'
'OK. You're forgiven,' says Dad. 'I'll just go over here and… Oops! Ahhh…'

That was it, over and over again. People ate it up. We love patterns. The much-celebrated Monty Python's Flying Circus sketch comedy group bases many of its successful scenes on setting and repeating patterns. In the famous 'Argument' sketch the characters simply contradict each other, saying, 'Yes, it is.' 'No, it's not.' The longer the pattern continues, the funnier the sketch becomes. On a primitive level the confirmation of our expectations pleases us.

Making connections

One way that improvisers practise making connections is by taking three unrelated words and stringing them together into a story. Try it. Here are your three words: 'book', 'marmalade' and 'leap'. (Coming up with three unrelated words taxes the mind at least as much as creating a story, by the way. Another Johnstonian exercise asks a pair of improvisers to take turns stating unrelated words until someone notices a connection. The game almost never goes more than four or five words before some relationship is evident.) Now, make up a story. You have 60 seconds. Go.

Here is what I came up with (the following is an unedited transcription of the story I improvised):

> Once upon a time there was a bear who loved two things: *books* and *marmalade*. Every day he would sit curled up in bed with his Big Book of Stories on his lap, and his paw in a jar of sweet and sticky orange marmalade. He never went anywhere. He didn't need to. His books transported him to far-off places of intrigue and romance, while at the same time his bed allowed him to feel safe and warm, and the marmalade sated his hunger and stimulated his senses. One day, however, something terrible happened. The marmalade from his paw had, after constant flipping of the pages, made them so sticky that they were impossible to part. The book became impossible to open. The bear panicked. What would he do now? Should he get up? No, he thought, he was too comfortable. And for a while he sat there sucking marmalade and staring out the window. Without the stories, though, to occupy his mind, he grew bored. He looked out the window and saw other bears in the distance. 'I wonder what they're doing out there.' The bed was still safe and the marmalade still sweet, so he stayed, but soon the marmalade disappeared – without the book to distract him he ate it up fast. With no stories and no marmalade, there was no choice. As scary as it was, the little bear made the *leap*. He left his bed and headed out into the world to find new adventure, new sweetness and whatever else might be in store.

How did it go for you? Was it easier than you expected? More difficult? Where did you get stuck? Were you aware of censoring yourself? What surprised you? Wasn't it satisfying to hear the words reincorporated? How did you decide what should happen next?

What happens next?

Let's take a look at that last question. 'What happens next?' is the funda-mental storytelling question. It provokes action. One way to create a story is simply to ask that question. Johnstone (1979) has a simple narrative game called 'What comes next?' In it, one actor behaves as the puppet, and other improvisers tell him or her what to do. Here is an example:

> The first actor asks, 'What comes first?'
> They tell her. 'You pick up a newspaper.'
> She does, and says, 'What comes next?'
> 'You see a picture of your long-lost husband.' She does.
> 'What comes next?' she asks.
> 'You read the story next to it, which says he was discovered on a desert island.'
> 'What comes next?'
> 'The doorbell rings.'
> 'What comes next?'
> 'You answer the door.'
> 'What comes next?'
> 'Your husband is standing there.'
> And so on.

Three-word stories

Overview:
- In pairs, participant take turns creating stories, based on three unrelated words that their partners provide.

Improv topics:
- Storytelling
- Spontaneity
- Listening and awareness
- Accepting offers

Purpose:
- Creativity
- Communication
- Team building
- Review

Supplies:
- None

Time:
- 5–7 minutes

Number of players:
- Pairs

Game flow:
- Have participants get into pairs.
- Have them choose an A and a B.
- Person A gives Person B three unrelated words.
- Person B creates a short story (30 seconds to a minute long) incorporating those three words.
- Participants switch roles.
- Debrief.

Variations:
- As a review activity, use words or concepts from the course.
- As a problem-solving activity, have the participants incorporate the words into an improvised solution.
- Have participants offer each other four or five words.

Tips:
- Demonstrate the process in front of the group, if participants are reticent.
- Remind participants that anything they say is correct.
- Use as a warm-up for story spine activities or in conjunction with the story spine.

Suggested debrief questions:
- How did you feel about your own story?
- How did you feel about your partner's story?
- What was easy about this? What was difficult?
- What makes a story a story? How did you know the story was over?
- What strategy did you employ to incorporate the words into your story?
- How did you choose the words for your partner?
- How is this like collaborating in real life?
- What did you learn about creativity?

Source:
- Keith Johnstone

At a slightly more complex level, a story results from establishing a routine and then breaking it. Johnstone (1979) explains this in terms of establishing 'platforms' or boring, familiar situations, and then introducing a 'tilt' or surprising shift. Del Close and Charna Halpern talk about setting up a relationship and an environment and then introducing some kind of 'event' that changes the status quo (Halpern, Close and Johnson, 1994). Although the language is different, the concept is the same. (For more information on these philosophies, consult *Truth in Comedy* (Halpern, Close and Johnson, 1994) and *Impro* (Johnstone, 1979).)

The story spine

At Freestyle Rep, Kenn Adams explored the nature of story structure even more specifically. Through his work in creating full-length narratives, Adams developed a number of tools to aid improvisers in building stories with well-made beginnings, middles and ends. Among these is a template that we at StoryNet have christened the 'story spine'. Story spine has become valued not only by improvisers but by keynote speakers, CEOs, advertising departments, screenwriters and trainers worldwide. It goes like this:

Once upon a time...
Every day...
But one day...
Because of that...
Because of that...
Because of that... (Repeat as needed.)
Until finally...
Ever since then...
And the moral of the story is... (optional).

This template builds in a platform, a change and consequences, and a resolution. Virtually all stories, at least in Western culture, possess this structure. When a story does not fulfil this model, we feel unsettled. Sometimes the storyteller deliberately skips a piece – like leaving a chord progression unresolved – to create tension and provoke thought. Sometimes, pieces are left out unintentionally and we are left unsatisfied. Either way, if the storyteller does not complete the structure, listeners will do so in their own mind. People in the United States are especially fond of stories that straightforwardly fulfil the story spine structure. Compare the French film *La Femme Nikita* with the US remake, *Point of No Return*. The second follows the structure much more rigidly, whereas the French version leaves some narrative connections ambiguous.

Here is a more detailed analysis of the story spine, and an example of a story you might recognize, mapped into it:

'Once upon a time...'
This is the introduction to the setting and characters in the story – the platform or the exposition. It gives listeners the context and sets the stage.

Example:
'Once upon a time, in the same city, there were two prominent families who despised each other.'

'Every day...'
The platform continues and develops.

Example:
'Every day the families feuded, fought and killed each other's members.'

'But one day...'
This is the catalyst, the reason the story is being told – why today is different.

Example:
'But one day, the son of one of the families crashed the birthday party of the other's daughter.'

'Because of that...' (Repeat at will.)
This is the heart of the story, the consequences that ensue from the catalyst. Each event leads to another event, building suspense and tension.

Examples:
'Because of that, the son and daughter fell in love.'
'Because of that, they secretly married.'
'Because of that, the son wanted the killing to stop.'
'Because of that, he stepped into the middle of a fight and inadvertently caused the death of his best friend.'
'Because of that, in agony and rage, he killed the killer, his wife's cousin.'
'Because of that, he was banished.'
'Because of that, the lovers needed to employ a complicated plan to be reunited.'
'Because the plan was complicated and depended on other people, communication broke down.'
'Because the message didn't get to him, the son didn't realize his wife was only faking her death, and he thought she was really dead when he found her in the family tomb.'
'Because of that, he killed himself.'

'Until finally...'
Here is the climax, the moment for which we all wait!

Example:
'Until finally, the daughter awoke to find her husband dead beside her, and she plunged his knife into her body, just as the members of both families entered the tomb to find their beloved children dead.'

'And ever since then...'
This is the resolution, the conclusion.

Example:
'And ever since then, both families have stopped the nonsensical war between them and have learnt to cooperate and live happily together.'
And the moral of the story is: feuds are stupid.

Adding flesh to the bones

Adams builds a complete structure to guide the storyteller through the different elements of a story plot. Of course, there is more to great storytelling than just what happens next. My retelling, above, of *Romeo and Juliet* was OK, but it certainly was not Shakespeare. Why not? As a matter of fact, why have all the versions of *Romeo and Juliet,* pre- and post-Shakespeare, been considered inferior to his? Shakespeare did an excellent job of structuring his version. All of the events build on each other, creating the inevitable end. However, the distinguishing element is not action, but description.

Shakespeare writes exquisitely beautiful language. His characters are robust, heart-wrenching and entertaining. His environments echo and support the emotional action. We all know that Shakespeare qualifies as the master of English theatre. Perhaps no one will ever challenge his genius. But we can enhance our stories through adding character and colour to our narrative skeletons.

My favourite exercise for weaving description into a plot is 'Colour/advance'. It came to me via Freestyle Repertory Theatre, and I believe it was originally based on a Viola Spolin exercise. 'Colour/advance' works like this. One player begins to tell a story. Periodically, a partner coaches the first player to 'colour' or describe some aspect of the story (eg a physical object, an emotion, an action). When the coach is satisfied, he or she calls, 'Advance', and the storyteller continues the action of the story. Here is an example:

> *Storyteller:* Once upon a time there was a sales manager named Stewart.
> *Coach:* Colour Stewart.
> *Storyteller:* Stewart had been in his position for 26 years and he was tired. He weighed 25 stones, ate two double cheeseburgers every day for lunch and wore a flea-bitten toupee.
> *Coach:* Advance.
> *Storyteller:* Every day Stewart took out his frustration on the sales-people who reported to him. He yelled at them, he overworked them and he undermined their effectiveness.
> *Coach:* Colour 'undermining their effectiveness'.
> *Storyteller:* Stewart would go along on sales calls and interrupt his sales-people, make fun of their technique and ask potential customers out on dates.
> *Coach:* Advance.
> *Storyteller:* One day, Stewart arrived at work to find a summons from the director of sales on his voice mail…
> And we will leave Stewart here to whatever his fate may be.

Colour/advance

Overview:
● This activity helps flesh out the details of a story, and balances description with action.

Improv topics:
● Storytelling
● Accepting offers
● Listening and awareness
● Spontaneity

Purpose:
● Creativity
● Communication
● Needs assessment
● Problem solving
● Review

Supplies:
● A flip chart, slide or handout with the story spine recorded

Time:
● 5–15 minutes

Number of players:
● Pairs

Game flow:
● Divide participants into pairs.
● Ask each pair to choose a storyteller and a guide.
● The storyteller begins to tell a story.
● Periodically the guide stops the storyteller and says, 'Colour the -', instructing the storyteller to enhance some detail. ('Colour' includes any kind of description – physical details, mood, inner thoughts and feelings of the characters.)
● When the guide is satisfied, he or she coaches, 'Advance', and the storyteller continues with the action of the story. ('Action' consists of anything that answers the question, 'What comes next?')
● Continue until the story is finished or time is up.
● Switch roles.

(Note: some trainers may wish to demonstrate this activity with a volunteer before having the pairs begin. If so, it is best for the facilitator to take the role of guide.)

Variations:
- Divide the participants into groups of three with two guides – one in charge of calling for colour, one in charge of advancing.
- Have the participants write their stories individually, arbitrarily calling out 'Colour' and 'Advance' from the front of the room.
- 'Conducted colour/advance'. Ask for three volunteers to tell a story. Assign one to be in charge of action, one in charge of physical description and one in charge of inner emotions and thoughts. Conduct the story by pointing to each person and have him or her continue the story focusing on his or her task. (See 'Conducted narrative', p 136.)
- Teach workshop participants the 'Colour/advance' vocabulary and allow them to colour and advance your lectures.

Tips:
- Coach the guides to limit their input to saying 'Colour' or 'Advance.' They should not ask questions (eg 'What's inside the box?') or offer suggestions (eg 'He marries the waitress, right?').
- Let the guides know that they can coach 'Colour' or 'Advance' for two reasons: to help the story or to 'work' the storyteller.
- Remind storytellers that part of the value of the exercise is to be able to distinguish between description and action, and that they should commit to doing one or the other, without moving on until they are coached.

Suggested debrief questions:
- Coaches, how did you decide when to call 'Colour' and 'Advance'?
- Storytellers, how did it feel to be led?
- Was one activity easier than the other?
- What sorts of items did you colour?
- How did the action and the description feed each other?
- How compelling were the stories that your partners told?
- How many of you feel like you are better storytellers than you thought?

Source:
- Adapted from Viola Spolin and Freestyle Repertory Theatre

Again, here are the main principles of story creation:

- Reincorporate.
- Build a strong structure, one that has a beginning, middle and end, that builds on itself, that establishes why today is different from any other, that piques interest and resolves questions (or deliberately sets up a question for people to ponder).
- Add flesh to the bones. Include description. Decorate the action with emotion, character and detail.

Using these storytelling techniques, improvisers produce rich and stimulating narratives. You can, too, and live happily ever after.

Application

As we discussed, virtually all information is processed through the development of narratives that link new content to other data and past experiences. When we can make the process of narrative creation conscious, our training and management effectiveness sky-rockets. Specifically, use stories and storytelling activities in the ways indicated in the following sections.

Pique interest

In 'By the first 30 seconds', an article in *Alaska Airlines Magazine*, Leonard Navarro quotes motivational speaker Rick Barrera. "'When you think of any compelling speaker," says Barrera, "you think of someone who can really tell a story to engage an audience and relate that to solid content. Stories make the content interesting.'" No matter how brilliant your information is, if people are not engaged, they will not absorb it. Stories can be used to break the ice, establish credibility and empathy, or frame the intention of a policy. They can add humour, suspense and drama. Look for opportunities to tell stories at every turn.

Use stories for introductions

Another reason that stories are such a powerful communication tool is that they are dynamic. The story resides as much in the mind of the listener as in the mouth of the teller. Students become more involved in their own learning when they engage in a story – even if it is just listening to one – rather than being asked to receive rote facts.

Supplying opportunities for others – students or team members – to share their own stories has added benefits. As a form of introduction, stories communicate more personal and memorable information than mere statistics, such as title, years of experience and objectives. In addition to telling the story of their name, as above, some examples of stories that participants may share include:

- pivotal stories from their work life;
- their most exciting adventure;
- how they arrived at the workshop – starting from birth, the first day at the company or that morning.

Assess needs

Stories can provide information about learners' expectations, previous knowledge and applicable skills. Workshop participants themselves may not be aware of all of the intricacies of their needs and relative experience. Through stories, trainers can gather robust and relatively complete data about learners' pedagogical and personal needs. Some specific ways to elicit this information include having participants:

- tell the story of what they got out of the workshop at the beginning of the session, as if it were over;
- share a true story of a great success they have had in order to gather best practices and tips to share;
- relate a story of frustration or disappointment as a way of determining some specific objectives and challenges.

Another way to assess needs through storytelling techniques is to modify the 'Colour/advance' activity described above. Teach the 'Colour/advance' vocabulary to the group, and allow people to prompt 'Colour' or 'Advance' as you lecture, if they need more detail or want to move on. This enables participants to express their needs at the time as you present.

Finally, stories need not be formally incorporated into training designs in order to provide clues to the needs of the learners. Listening to the stories people tell at breaks and probing for stories when questions come up are also excellent ways of harvesting needs.

Increase retention

Because learning is innately a storytelling process, the conscious use of storytelling activities assists in the process of retention. As review activities, you may:

- have participants – individually or in groups – create a story that illustrates a learning point or principle;
- provide a story that illustrates a process or incorporates data as a mnemonic device;
- have participants write the 'story of the workshop' as a way of assessing retention and evaluating understanding.

When asking participants to create stories, Adams's story spine has proven to be an excellent tool. The structure works as a guide and tends to relieve whatever pressure individuals might feel to tell 'good' stories. If you are asking people to work collaboratively, the spine also helps to align the efforts.

Enrich visioning and problem solving

Traditional visioning activities can result in beautiful pictures, but often leave the path to those Elysian Fields murky. Through the use of storytelling, groups are able to flesh out the process as well as the goal. Again, the story spine works in this context. If the 'vision' is the happy ending, the 'ever since then', what is the story that got us from here to there? What obstacles were overcome? How did the team members contribute?

Another story format that can be adapted to problem-solving sessions is Joseph Campbell's hero's journey. The hero's journey is an analysis of the ubiquitous quest structure found in works as disparate as *Star Wars*, Homer's *Odyssey* and *Crouching Tiger, Hidden Dragon*. A breakdown of the formula can be found in Campbell's own *A Hero with a Thousand Faces* (1973), as well as in storytelling and screenwriting books, including Christopher Vogler's *The Writer's Journey* (1998).

Build teams

People in the United States who have been to summer camp may remember how bonded they and their friends felt. There was nothing like hanging around a campfire singing songs and exchanging ghost stories. Somehow other relationships never felt as satisfying and intense. All the ways that we have discussed so far to improve teamwork – getting to know each other better, enhancing empathy, building on each other's ideas, listening well – live in storytelling activities. The effect is enhanced when the group creates stories together. It hardly matters what the content of the stories is. Whenever there is an opportunity to share stories or invent them collaboratively, we recommend it.

Key points

- Storytelling is a historical, current and profound learning tool.
- Stories are the heart of theatre and the heart of communication.
- Approaches to narrative vary, but share some fundamental theories.
- The difference between a list of events and a story is connectivity.
- Reincorporating is the foundation of a story.
- 'What happens next' is a fundamental question of stories.
- Stories establish a routine and then break it.
- The story spine defines the structure of a well-made story.
- Detail enhances the action of a story and makes it more compelling.
- Pique interest through stories.
- Use stories for introductions.
- Assess needs.
- Increase retention.
- Enrich visioning activities.
- Build teams.

7

Non-verbal communication

It is a known fact that the human body and psychology influence each other and are in constant interplay.

Michael Chekhov (1953)

...the most important thing that the storyteller has to consider in non-verbal communication is that of 'congruence', that is making sure that what you say is being backed up by what you do or how you appear.

Margaret Parkin (1998)

The principle

Improvisers take on three roles whenever they step on stage. Simultaneously, they function as actors, directors and writers. The writer third of the improviser can easily fall into the trap of 'telling not showing'. As playwrights know, behaviour trumps words in impact. (You know what they say about the relative value of pictures and words.) Still, because we are so much more conscious of the words we use, it is easy to forget that communication depends on so many non-verbal cues. A number of the exercises that Spolin created are silent – no words allowed – for just this reason. In one exercise, improvisers pair up to do a scene with only one person able to speak. Observers and the players alike find that the mute improviser has just as much power to make offers and further the action of the scene as the verbal one. When improvisers are forced to relinquish their language skills, they see how much they can communicate with their bodies.

There are three aspects of the non-verbal work in improv that are useful outside of the theatrical world. They are: forging a strong and supple instrument, aligning the mind and the body, and status. Let's take them one by one.

The person, the instrument

Most artists use tools external to themselves. Painters have their brushes and canvases; writers have their pens and paper; musicians have their keyboards, trumpets or violins. What actors have is themselves. A significant portion of acting training is spent in movement, voice and speech classes. The concept is that, no matter how much you feel or how brilliant the words you speak are, if you do not have a strong 'instrument', you will not be able to communicate the beauty of the music. Great musicians invest large sums of money in Stradivarius violins. Actors are stuck with whatever body they are born with, and they must transform it into a precious instrument.

Improvisers depend on their bodies and voices to be both strong and flexible. In the course of a two-hour show, they may play a dozen distinct characters. Each character, while looking, moving and sounding different (all without costumes and props, mind you), must be comfortably seen and heard by the audience. That requires physical stamina and agility. The exercises designed to build those skills are straightforward. Developing a strong instrument involves ongoing conditioning and practice. Like athletes, the best improvisers work out regularly, and warm up before game time.

What is true on stage is just as true when running a workshop, giving a sales presentation or motivating a team. Your body should be relaxed and open, your voice should be audible and pleasant, and both should convey the feelings and intent behind your words.

Conditioning your instrument

In addition to this general conditioning, there are specific techniques that performers learn to adapt their behaviours to stage or screen. Stage actors practise projecting their voices and extending their gestures to fill unnaturally large spaces, for example. Film and television actors learn to reduce extraneous movements, since the camera will exaggerate them.

Increasingly, those in the corporate world find they must acquire performance skills. Businesses host annual meetings for audiences of thousands. Sales-people give presentations to clients across the world via teleconferencing technology. And the pressure to present well continues to increase. The public has become acutely conditioned by television, and judges as much on appearance as on substance.

Dennis Miller, a caustic US comedian and talk-show host, has a famous rant about the fun most people in the United States made of Ross Perot's running mate, Admiral James Stockdale, after his appearance in the 1992 vice-presidential debate. The admiral was a kind and respected intellectual with a distinguished military record. He also happened to be uncomfortable on camera. As Miller says, Stockdale committed the only unpardonable sin of our culture. He looked bad on television.

Aligning mind and body

Training the body in the ways discussed above is easy, and relatively common in presentation and media training courses. Another area of non-verbal training revolves around the connection between the body and the mind. Kirk Livingston, the current artistic director of Bay Area Theatresports, told me that the most important thing he has learnt in his non-verbal training is that 'the body is always in the present, whereas the mind floats around in the past and the future'. In other words, if we wish to be spontaneous and aware, our physical selves are the key to success. Our bodies have no choice. They must be in the moment. For the most part, they cannot whisk themselves out of the room if they feel threatened or shy. Our minds do that all the time. Our bodies cannot be in two places at once. Many of us are in three or four places at the same time mentally. What Livingston suggests, then, is that our bodies are more reliable than our minds. They are more in touch with the reality around them and therefore a better guide to making real connections.

As babies, we are completely integrated. When we feel a physical sensation, we cry out with deep emotion until we are comfortable again. When we are angry or sad, we scrunch up our bodies and faces and turn bright red as we cry. We sleep when we are tired, without worrying about what will happen tomorrow.

As we get older, we separate our thoughts from our immediate physical sensations. One of the ways we do this is by tensing our muscles and holding our breath to cut off the connection. That is why babies make much clearer, louder crying sounds than adults, even though they are so much smaller. But as much as we may want to separate mind and body, the two affect each other. Some of the most progressive businesses have begun to invite masseurs into their offices for just this reason. They realize that if their employees are physically comfortable and healthy, they will also feel more content and work more productively. A colleague of mine, who specializes in creative problem solving, advocates going for a walk when the solution to a problem has eluded you for a length of time. 'It is easier to change your body than to change your mind,' he says.

Individuals have comfort zones, and some people feel more in touch with their physicality, some with their feelings, some with their intellects. Athletes, for example, tend to have heightened sensitivity to and control over physical experience. Computer programmers tend to depend on their mental capabilities. I am reminded of my own tendency to depend on my cerebral capacities, when I interrupt my writing to perform. One night recently, I found myself focusing so much on my intellect – planning what I should say and analysing the scenes I was in – that I felt sluggish and uninspired. I would have gone home completely discouraged if I had not been called upon to play a pig in one scene.

As a pig, I could only communicate non-verbally. I had no words, just squeaks and eyes and little hooves. I was forced to be present and connected to my body. I am sure it was my most creative work of the night. Certainly the audience thought so.

Individuals in business settings tend to depend on their minds more than their bodies. Business professionals report that they spend much more time planning *what* they will say in presentations than they do practising *how* they will say it. The world of business is extremely abstract. However, as every actor knows, the same content can be delivered in a myriad of ways, creating deeply different effects. Albert Mehrabian, in his 1971 book *Silent Messages*, presents studies that confirm that we trust vocal and visual cues much more than we do verbal cues. His statistics say that when we decide whether or not to trust a message, and the verbal, tonal and visual cues are in conflict, we make our decision based on the following percentages: how the speaker looks – 55 per cent; how the speaker sounds – 38 per cent; what the speaker says – 7 per cent. At first, workshop participants express shock at this statistic. However, it is not really that surprising. Words come from our sophisticated, conscious brains. Our physical and vocal responses emanate from much more primitive, and therefore less controlled, places.

What this truth leads us to is the realization that, no matter how brilliant the content we have to deliver, if we do not get our bodies along for the ride, we have much less power to affect and convince our audience. Casting directors say that they make their decisions about the actors who audition for them within the first 15 seconds of their audition. They do not have to wait to hear how the monologue unfolds. They can tell from the way the actor looks, sounds, stands and moves whether he or she will fulfil their requirements. Similarly, the success of a trainer, salesperson or manager may be much more connected to how the message is delivered than we like to think.

For the same reasons that physical and vocal communication is powerful, students often confront it with discomfort and confusion. As soon as we engage our voices and bodies we become vulnerable. We must tear down the walls that have protected us. The reward we receive in exchange is an ability to affect and be affected. It is a valuable power, indeed. A number of the spontaneity and trust-building exercises in this book double as techniques for increasing physical comfort and awareness. The uneasiness that comes with the first forays into this area is more than worth the results.

Inside out/outside in

It is possible to develop from the outside in or the inside out. British acting training tends to work the first way and US the second. Sometimes, if students are struggling with their physicality, asking them to change their internal focus can help.

A couple of years ago, a colleague and I were hired by a major software company to train their new spokeswoman. She was to be their new 'human face', designed to make their image more attractive to the home consumer. Carey (not her real name) had already been exposed to media training, but she came to us nervous and confused. From her previous coach, she had learnt how to sit, how to stand and what not to say. What she had not learnt to do was behave authentically. During the two days that we were together, we had Carey practise telling stories from her own life, and talk about her own passions and desires. As she opened up, her face and body relaxed and, without thinking, she began to look more attractive, more convincing and easier to understand. For her, the key was internal connection, and the external behaviour took care of itself.

Whether you approach integration from the inside out or the outside in, the integration remains imperative. Just as a house divided against itself cannot stand, an instrument divided against itself cannot sing.

Status

'Status', in this context, is defined as power dynamics. The discussion of status has been placed in this chapter, because status is an ephemeral quality that permeates all aspects of human interaction. Verbal exchanges affect status, too, but they are a small part of the equation. Words, actions, clothing, title, knowledge all combine to define a person's status.

Status is not the same as official title or rank. In studying power, social science researchers have investigated different sources of power. They have then divided them into two classes, positional and personal. We make a mistake if we assume the two always go hand in hand. An ineffectual director may have less actual status than an efficient personal assistant.

As a way of looking at relationships and dramatic action, status entered the improvisational lexicon via the work of Keith Johnstone. I do not think it is a coincidence that Johnstone, a Briton, focused on the concept while none of his US counterparts did. People in the United States eschew the concept of class and power. If everyone is supposed to be created equal, that must mean everyone *is* equal. An awareness of status differences, especially within a small community or team, has come to constitute political incorrectness. Organizations flatten their hierarchies and expect that status differentials will disappear. And it is often those with the most power who resist the concept the most strongly. As social science tells us, the privileged are often blind to their privileges.

Other cultures show more awareness. Status exists – all the time, everywhere. What may distinguish one culture from another is which characteristics endow someone with status, which behaviours are expected of individuals with differing status roles and how stable those roles are. Johnstone's genius was to recognize that status can be understood not as something we *are*, but as something we *do* (1979). We confer or accept status through our behaviours, and it is those interactions that determine who is perceived as holding the power.

Johnstone (1979) found that when his students 'played' high or low status, their work on stage became richer and looked more like real-life behaviour. It is his focus on behaviours that signal high or low status that has proved so useful in communication-skills training. Through an exploration of these non-verbal cues, students heighten their perceptions of status relationships and learn to raise and lower their own and others' status. Peter Falk's detective character Columbo, for example, plays low status in order to confound murderers who often hold high-status positions. Ultimately, Columbo wins through his tenacity, brilliance and expertise, but in the meantime he tricks his adversaries into underestimating him, so that they let their guards down.

Drew Westen (1996) highlights our awareness of status roles when he summarizes the work of psychologists Levine and Moreland in this way: 'Humans, like other animals, usually have little difficulty reading signs of status and recognizing who defers to whom. People high in status in a group tend to talk more and are freer to interrupt. They also display their status non-verbally, by standing erect, maintaining eye contact longer, and generally displaying signs of confidence.' Johnstone adds that high-status individuals tend to move fluidly and hold their heads still. Low-status behaviours, he says, include making oneself small physically and vocally, saying 'um' and 'ah' a lot, touching one's face and hair, and trying to make eye contact but looking away quickly. The first set of behaviours signals calm and security; the second signals nervousness and a desire to please.

Playing with status highlights the power of non-verbal behaviours to change the sense of a message. In an exercise adapted from *Impro* (Johnstone, 1979), participants are given a short script of neutral dialogue and asked to play it over and over with different status relationships. The huge effect of a roll of the eyes or a giggle is stunning. Often, I will use a job-interview setting for the short scene written by the students. It might look something like this:

A: *Good morning.*
B: Good morning.
A: *Have a seat.*
B: Thank you.
A: *I have looked over your CV.*
B: Yes?
A: *I see you worked at Global Limited.*
B: Yes. For a number of years.
A: *Very impressive.*
B: Thanks.

Often, participants assume that the interviewer will have high status by default. All the actor playing the role must do, though, is sound impressed and eager to please, and the interviewee's status rises. Conversely, even a line like 'Very impressive' can seem cutting when said with a dismissive tone.

Because it is so fundamental to our social structures, our sensitivity to status is highly honed. 'Status cards' illustrates this awareness. Participants are given a playing card that they put on their foreheads without looking at the face. The card signifies their status, and the group treats each member accordingly. When they are asked to line up in order of status, based on how they were treated, most groups have over 90 per cent accuracy, and many individuals can guess their cards exactly.

Status cards

Overview:
- Participants are given a playing card that indicates their status. Each participant 'wears' the card on his or her forehead without knowing what it is. As if they are at an annual employee meeting, the participants treat each other with the status indicated by the card. At the end of the role-play, the group lines up in order of their perceived status.

Improv topics:
- Non-verbal behaviours
- Listening and awareness

Purposes:
- Warm-up
- Energy builder
- Team building
- Communication

Supplies:
- One deck of cards for every 52 people

Time:
- 10–20 minutes

Number of players:
- 5–100

Game flow:
- Distribute a playing card to each participant. Make sure that there is a variety of numbers – low to high.
- Instruct the participants not to look at their cards as you pass them out.
- Have the group place the cards face out on their foreheads, still without looking at their own cards.
- Set up a role-play. Explain that the group is at an annual company meeting. Each person should be treated with the status indicated by his or her card. (Aces are high; twos are low.) As the players get clues about their status, they should take on the behaviours that are associated with it.
- After a few minutes of mingling, ask the participants to form a line with the lowest card at one end and the highest at the other. Participants should place themselves where they think they belong, still refraining from looking at their own cards.

- If there are fewer than 20 players, ask each one to guess his or her card out loud.
- Invite the players to look at their cards.
- Debrief.

Variations:
- Set up a different scenario for the role-play (eg an office party, an awards ceremony, Santa's workshop at the North Pole, a board meeting).
- Play without words.
- Play more than one round, so that each person gets to experience more than one position.
- Play a round in which people see their own card, and not the others.
- Play a round in which everyone sees all the cards.

Tips:
- Status is touchy. Leave lots of time for discussion.
- You may wish to play 'Status demo' (see page 174) or 'Status pass' (see page 176) before this activity to introduce the concept of status, and illustrate high- and low-status behaviours.
- You may wish to follow up with 'Neutral status scene' (see page 153).
- Remind people many times to refrain from looking at their cards.

Suggested debrief questions:
- What kind of signals did you get as to your status?
- What kind of signals did you give?
- How did it feel to be very high? Very low? In the middle?
- Who were you most comfortable talking to?
- What assumptions did you make about people with different statuses?
- Those of you who did not guess your cards, why not? What signals did you get? What internal assumptions did you make?
- How did you feel when other people behaved in ways that contradicted their assigned status?
- How is this like real life?

Source:
- Adapted from Matt Smith, Rebecca Stockley and Seattle Theatresports

Not only are we aware of status, but the desire for it is an exceptionally strong motivator. Keith Allred, currently a professor at the Kennedy School of Government, Harvard University, and an expert in negotiation theory, stated in one of his classes at Columbia University that people will give up tangible gains – like money – in exchange for status (1996). And, he says, they will reject agreements that are clearly in their best interests if they feel as though they are not getting the respect they deserve. It makes sense that status wields such influence in human interactions. Historically, the person with the highest status got the best food and the most opportunities to procreate. (That is probably still true, though the attributes that confer status may have changed.)

In addition to being behavioural, status is also dynamic. You may have high status in one situation (for example, giving a presentation) and low status in another (fixing your computer). Think about your family. Who has the highest status when it comes to making decisions about money? How do you know? What behaviours does that person engage in that signal he or she has the status? How about when it comes to deciding which film to see or what to serve for dinner? Does the same person have the status?

In my co-worker Mandy's family, her mother has always controlled the financial aspects of her family's life. Her mother is extremely generous and not visibly controlling, but her status is clear. Mandy's father actually makes more money, but he deposits it in a joint bank account and goes to his wife when he wishes to make a major purchase. She has the power. There are a number of reasons that her mother holds this status. The main one is she loves to manage the money. Her husband doesn't care to. In this situation, he has the positional power as the breadwinner, but she has status stemming from her knowledge, expertise and passion.

Now consider your organization. What attributes confer the most status on individuals there? Title? Expertise? Age? Gender? Knowledge? Affiliation? In which situations do you feel you have status? Are there situations in which you would like to have more? Less?

Not only cultures but individuals can have varying status preferences. Johnstone said, in *Impro* (1979), that he believed, 'that people have a preferred status; that they like to be low, or high, and that they try to manoeuvre themselves into the preferred position'. A colleague of mine, for example, claims that she prefers to be the second in command. There is always someone else to go to for help, to learn from and to pass the buck to. Yet she has affiliative power, and enough status to be included in important decisions and exciting activities. Where do you think you are most comfortable? What about each of your managers? Your trainees? Does it change with the situation?

The benefits of status awareness

Business people and performers benefit from status awareness in contradictory ways. Status awareness benefits performers in two major ways.

First, the best performers are said to have an ability to 'take the stage'. They exude a charisma whose source is elusive. Developing a strong and flexible body and voice helps to build this vibrancy. And yet, there seems to be something more. Finding ways to claim status may be part of it. Additionally, much dramatic action revolves around shifts in status between characters or between a character and society. *Oedipus Rex*, for example, chronicles the rise and fall of its title character from the lowest position of abandoned child to the highest royalty and back to devastated beggar. Much of Shakespeare similarly explores the rise and fall of kings. The story of David and Goliath has delighted readers for years with its description of the weak overcoming the strong, tipping the status balance. Many US classics recount the story of a low-status character attempting to achieve the American Dream – acquire money and fame and hence status. Improvisers, actors and playwrights study status, because it helps them create drama. Changes in status make for compelling action on stage.

Trainers and managers working in business settings find status awareness useful for the opposite reason. By learning to equalize status, they can enhance communication and motivation. Remember the trust formula? If the status gap gets too big, people do not believe that leaders can empathize with them, so they do not feel safe. And a leader, if separated from people by too big a status gap, fails to get important information and advice.

Through an awareness of status interactions, trainers can raise the status of their learners to facilitate participation and comfort. Or they can raise their own status to focus the group. Managers can set effective limits, or seem more accessible. Individual contributors can increase the possibility that their ideas will be heard and valued. Sales-people can connect with their clients, children can appease their parents and couples can resolve sticky issues that they might not have understood before. For a further discussion of the topic, consult *Impro* (Johnstone, 1979) or, for an academic approach, look to French and Raven's seminal work (1959) on social power dynamics.

As we strengthen our physical and vocal instrument, align our bodies with our minds and raise our awareness of the effects of our behaviours, we augment our communicative prowess. It is not a fluke that our political and community leaders are increasingly being drawn from the ranks of performers.

Application

When the business community first began to turn to theatre professionals, it was for presentation-skills and media training. It is no trick to translate theatrical techniques to the performance aspects of business communication.

As I am sure you have already discovered, there is more to it than that.

The behavioural, vocal and status-based exercises included in this book provide guidelines for developing skills that business professionals often ignore. They are suitable both as workshop activities and as personal development tools. Apply them in the ways detailed in the following sections.

Enhance presentation skills

The most straightforward application of this non-verbal work is presentation skills. The trainer standing in front of a classroom or the sales manager giving a report needs to be seen and understood, and needs to inspire confidence and enthusiasm. Whenever people present in a formal situation, the effects of their gestures and vocal tones are magnified. A habitual gesture that may not be noticeable one to one can loom large on the stage. The time to think about the non-verbal aspects of a presentation is not during the presentation. There are plenty of other things to focus on then. Strengthen your voice and body ahead of time through regular exercise, and spend as much time planning the form of your presentation as you do planning the content. (Form, by the way, includes not only your physical and vocal work, but also all of the 'set and costume' trappings. What do your slides look like? Is your handwriting legible? What are you going to wear?)

Align the mind and the body

Since the body and the mind are connected, they affect each other. This is hardly news for those of you who have lain awake at night worrying about a project or relationship. The good news is that by taking care of our bodies we can relieve stress and increase productivity. During a presentation, for example, taking the time to breathe slowly and deeply can reduce nervousness as well as its physical manifestations.

A strong body can also help a trainer maintain concentration and energy throughout a training session. When the body gets tired so does the brain. An eight-hour day constitutes an awfully long performance. Even with breaks, it requires physical as well as mental stamina.

In a related vein, the more healthy and alert your body is, the more attuned you can be to the environment, and, as we know, listening and awareness enhance both creativity and communication. In addition to the external environment, your own body will give you useful data. If you feel hungry, perhaps your students do as well. If your insides feel tense, perhaps there is some sort of conflict that you need to resolve. Take care of your body and then listen to what it tells you.

Make conscious status choices

An ability to manipulate status dynamics is a potent tool. As noted, the more equalized the status, the smoother the communication. Facilitation, mediation, negotiation and presentation skills all depend to some degree or another on this capacity. A trainer may choose to raise the status of his or her students to increase their sense of control and feeling of competence, for example. This can be achieved through an action as subtle as sitting rather than standing, or one as blatant as turning over the position of teacher to a participant. A new manager may choose to change his or her gestures and vocal patterns to sound more confident, and therefore credible, when speaking to the managing director. A coach can pay attention to the subtle signs of high or low status in the person being coached, and adjust in order to keep communication flowing.

When experimenting with status, here are a couple of tips to keep in mind. First, inauthentic behaviour will be spotted and backfire. Our animal sense is keen. The power here resides in aligning behavioural signals with our intentions. If the two are not aligned, the results can be ineffective, embarrassing or, at worst, unethical. Second, the qualities that bestow status on someone vary widely from environment to environment. What one wears in a law firm to garner high status is not the same as one wears on a football field – or at a dot-com, for that matter. The same holds true for vocabulary, story, and pedagogical and managerial choices. Know your audience. What will they identify with? Which stylistic choices are they used to? What is their preferred status relationship?

If you are conscious, aligned and authentic, your non-verbal behaviours can catapult your effectiveness to increasingly higher levels of mastery. And that is more than just words.

Key points

- Non-verbal behaviour often carries more weight than the verbal communication.
- Three aspects of non-verbal behaviour from theatrical work are:
    - forging a strong body;
    - aligning the mind and body;
    - status.
- An actor's (or presenter's) body is his or her instrument.
- Giving a presentation is like being on stage.
- We focus more on content then on form, even though form is so important, because developing our voices and bodies can be uncomfortable at first.

- Status is defined as power dynamics.
- Status can be viewed as something we do, not something we are.
- Status is fluid and variable.
- Status comes from a variety of personal and positional criteria, including non-verbal behaviours.
- Personal and positional status positions are not always aligned.
- We are very attuned to, and motivated by, status.
- Individuals may have preferred status roles.
- The more equal the status, the more communication is facilitated.

Section 2

Additional activities

Beware of FUN-phobia – it's better to get there laughing than to get nowhere bored.

van Hauen, Kastberg and Soden

There is a final principle of the theatre that must be included for our discussion to be complete. Underlying everything we have spoken about so far is the idea of 'serving the scene'. To serve the scene means simply to add what is needed when it is needed. Different moments require different tools. Directors say that casting is 90 per cent of their job. The right actor for one role might sabotage a production in another. Actors must learn both to take and to give focus depending on their role and the style and narrative journey of a particular play. In an improvised show, the performers must discern when to jump into a scene and when to hold back, what type of game to introduce to support the dramatic arc of the show and how to interact with different types of audiences. No one strategy works all the time.

As trainers and managers, we, too, must vary our styles and techniques. One choice is when and how to introduce interactive activities. Perhaps you will choose to do so more frequently now. Another is which activities to use to achieve which goals.

This section was designed to provide a large body of activities, complete with variations and debrief points that can be adapted for wide-ranging goals and environments. Each of the previous chapters has included sample activities for the chapter topic. They, along with these additional activities, can in fact be used to explore many of the principles we have discussed.

As I mentioned in the Introduction, *Training Using Drama* does not purport to be a comprehensive compilation of theatre games. The exercises I have included are those I have found to offer the most value to individuals training and working in business settings. In writing the game descriptions, I have assumed that the reader possesses a certain level of facilitation experience. My goal was to provide enough material about each activity for the trainer to understand the flow and applications of each game. Depending on the focus of the training, different variations and debrief questions will prove most useful.

There are often a number of variations included within each exercise description. Some of these are simple modifications, whereas other variations could qualify as separate activities. I have identified the exercises in terms of their training and theatrical topics. As for the origins of each activity, let me reiterate. I have done my best to attribute each game accurately, though the task was made difficult by the oral nature of our art form, and the years of cross-pollination among theatre and improv organizations. The descriptions are my adaptations and articulations of exercises gleaned from a variety of sources. I have done my best to attribute the games to the sources of which I am aware.

Finally, feel free to adapt these exercises, and use them for purposes other than those specified here. After all, that kind of innovation is what the theatre is all about.

Ask a silly question

Overview:
- Quickly fire off silly questions and call on participants to answer them as spontaneously as they can. Examples are: 'What does an elephant wear to bed?' 'How do people cook spaghetti on Mars?' 'Why does a bear snore?' There are no wrong answers, save not saying something.

Improv topics:
- Spontaneity
- Accepting offers
- Trust

Purpose:
- Ice-breaker
- Warm-up
- Energy builder
- Team building
- Creativity

Supplies:
- None

Time:
- 3–8 minutes

Number of players:
- Various

Game flow:
- Tell the participants that you are going to quiz them.
- The good news is that anything they say is right.
- Ask silly questions and encourage the respondents to answer as quickly as possible, saying whatever comes to mind. Some sample questions are:
  - How do you turn bubblegum into gold?
  - Why do monkeys play the cymbals?
  - Why is the moon made of cheese?
  - What are the three friendliest colours?
  - What do you mush in a mushroom?

Variations:
- Have participants play in pairs, or groups of three or four, taking turns asking and answering questions.
- Play in a circle with each person giving a question to the person on his or her right.
- Hand out a written sheet of questions and have a competition for the participant who can finish first. Then have everyone share answers.

Tips:
- Coach participants to answer quickly and say anything.
- Ask open-ended questions, rather than ones that elicit 'Yes' or 'No' answers.
- The sillier the question, the better. Participants will be more willing to be spontaneous if it is very clear that there are no 'right' answers.
- As the facilitator, you may want to create some silly questions ahead of time. It may be significantly harder to come up with silly questions than to answer them.

Suggested debrief questions:
- What happened when I told you there would be a quiz?
- How did you feel when I said any answer was right?
- How did you censor yourself?
- What felt good?
- What is the value of saying the first thing that comes to mind?
- What is the value of asking silly questions?

Source:
- Adapted from Kenn Adams and Freestyle Repertory Theatre

Awareness quiz

Overview:
- Participants begin by having a short conversation in pairs. Then they stand with their backs to their partners and their eyes closed. The facilitator asks questions about the partners' appearance, which people answer silently to themselves. Then the pairs turn to each other and check their observational accuracy.

Improv topic:
- Listening and awareness

Purpose:
- Warm-up
- Energy builder
- Team building
- Creativity
- Communication

Supplies:
- None

Time:
- 3–5 minutes

Number of players:
- Pairs

Game flow:
- Have each participant find a partner.
- Ask them to introduce themselves or have a short conversation. (One possible topic is to find two or three things that they have in common that they did not already know about.)
- Have the pairs stand back to back with their eyes closed.
- Ask the following questions and have the participants answer silently to themselves:
  - What kind of shoes is your partner wearing? What colour are they? How do they fasten? Can you see your partner's socks? If so, what do they look like? Is your partner wearing socks at all?
  - What is your partner wearing on the bottom? Trousers? A skirt? What colour? Material? How does it fasten? Is your partner wearing a belt?

- – What kind of shirt is your partner wearing? Colour? Material? What's the neckline like? Are there buttons? What are the sleeves like?
- – Is he or she wearing jewellery? What kind?
- – What is his or her hair like? Colour? Length? How is it fastened?
- – Is your partner wearing glasses? Does your partner have facial hair?
- – What colour are your partner's eyes?
- Once you have asked all the questions, have the partners turn around and check their accuracy.

Variations:
- Ask the participants questions about the environment. How many windows? What colour is the carpet? Etc.
- Ask the participants questions about their own watch.
- Practise individually by closing your eyes at various times and quizzing yourself on your observation of your desk phone, the bus you are on, your car dashboard, etc.
- Have the participants close their eyes for 60 seconds and note all the sounds that they hear.

Tips:
- When playing in pairs, you may wish to play the 'Classic mirror' exercise (page 134) before engaging in the 'Awareness quiz'.
- Coach the participants to remain silent during the exercise.
- Give the participants a few moments to chat with each other before debriefing as an entire group.

Suggested debrief questions:
- How did you do? Anyone get 100 per cent? Anyone get nothing?
- What kinds of things do we notice? Why?
- Why do we block out so much information?
- How do we decide what to pay attention to?
- How much better would you have done, had I asked you to study the other person ahead of time?
- What does this tell us about our powers of observation?
- How can we improve our levels of awareness?

Source:
- Adapted from Patricia Ryan, improv instructor, Stanford University, and David K Reynolds, PhD

Ball ball

Overview:
- The participants stand in a circle, tossing a soft volleyball around, attempting to keep it in the air for as long as possible. No one may tap the ball more than once in a row, and the ball may not touch the ground.

Improv topics:
- Accepting offers
- Listening and awareness
- Trust

Purpose:
- Ice-breaker
- Warm-up
- Energy builder
- Team building
- Communication
- Needs assessment
- Review
- Closing

Supplies:
- A soft ball

Time:
- 7–15 minutes

Number of players:
- 4–20

Game flow:
- Participants stand in a circle.
- One person tosses a ball into the air.
- Participants hit the ball to each other, keeping it from touching the ground for as long as possible. No one may hit the ball more than once in a row.
- Participants count the hits out loud as they go.

Variations:
- As a needs assessment activity, have participants shout out issues they have or things they would like to get from the training, rather than numbers.
- As a review activity, have the participants shout out learning points from the training.
- As a brainstorming activity, have the participants shout out ideas.
- Have the participants tell a story one word at a time, shouting out the word as they hit the ball.
- Play with two or three balls.

Tips:
- This simple game highlights the main skills of teamwork. You may wish to talk about 'hogging the ball', 'wimping out' and the variety of skills that help the team accomplish even such a simple goal.
- Find a soft ball that will not hurt people's hands or head. A ball the size of a soccer ball but softer is best.

Suggested debrief questions:
- What helped us to be successful?
- What hindered our process?
- How much were you willing to participate? Why?
- How did you feel when the team dropped the ball?
- How did you feel when you thought you were responsible? When someone else was?
- How did individuals support each other?
- How is this like real life?

Source:
- Rebecca Stockley and Bay Area Theatresports via Craig Turner, University of Washington, based on the work of Jacques LeCoq

Blindfold walk

Overview:
- In pairs, have the participants take turns leading and following. Followers close their eyes and the leaders guide them around the space without touching them, by calling their name.

Improv topics:
- Trust
- Listening and awareness
- Non-verbal communication

Purpose:
- Warm-up
- Team building
- Communication

Supplies:
- None

Time:
- 10–20 minutes

Number of players:
- Pairs

Game flow:
- Demonstrate this activity with a volunteer before engaging the entire group.
- Divide the participants into pairs.
- Have each pair choose an A and a B.
- Have the As close their eyes and the Bs lead them around the space by calling their name.
- Instruct the participants that the most important rule is that no one gets hurt, so they may say 'Stop' or touch their partners, if it looks as though their partners' safety is at risk. Otherwise they should refrain from saying anything but their partners' names.
- After a few minutes, have the As and Bs switch roles.

Variations:
- Have the leaders hold the hands of the followers, rather than call their names.

- Have the leaders use language.
- Have one leader with his or her eyes open, and two to four followers holding hands behind with their eyes closed.

Tips:
- Emphasize the safety and trust aspects of the game. Monitor the participants as they go.
- The more room there is to explore, the more interesting the game is. Allow participants to go outside the workshop room, if possible – through doorways, along halls, up and down stairs.

Suggested debrief questions:
- How did it feel to follow?
- How did it feel to lead?
- Which role were you more comfortable in?
- What did you explore?
- How many risks did you take?
- Did trust increase or decrease? Why?

Source:
- Adapted from Viola Spolin

But vs and

Overview:
- Two groups set about the task of planning a company party. The first must start each sentence with the words, 'Yes, but...'. The second must start sentences with the words, 'Yes, and...'. The first group will struggle to achieve anything. The second will create much more easily. (See page 46.)

Improv topics:
- Accepting offers
- Listening and awareness

Purpose:
- Team building
- Creativity
- Communication

Supplies:
- None

Time:
- 4–8 minutes

Number of players:
- Various

Game flow:
- Round 1
  - Ask for three to five volunteers.
  - Tell the group that they are in charge of planning the company holiday party.
  - Each person must contribute an idea. There is no specific order, but no one may contribute more than one idea in a row.
  - Anyone may start, and each successive idea must begin with the words, 'Yes, but...'.
  - Allow the exercise to continue for two to three minutes, or until it degenerates beyond repair.
- Round 2
  - Ask for three to five new volunteers.
  - Set up the same activity with the following adjustment.

- This time each new sentence must start with the words, 'Yes, and...'.
- Allow the activity to continue for two to three minutes or until the group seems satisfied and delighted.

Variations:
- Play simultaneously in pairs or groups of up to five people. Allow each group to try both the 'Yes, but...' and the 'Yes, and...' versions.
- Assign a different task, eg creating a meeting agenda or designing a new product.
- Have the same group of five people demonstrate both rounds.
- Role-play with some people saying 'Yes, and...' and some saying 'Yes, but...'.

Tips:
- Continue to remind participants to use the words, 'Yes, and...' or 'Yes, but...'.
- End the rounds when the ideas trail off (usually in the first round) or on an explosion of approval (usually the second round).
- Pay attention to the intention of the statements. If the demonstration does not work, it may be because the participants are actually blocking, even though they are saying 'Yes, and...', or vice versa.

Suggested debrief questions:
- How does it feel to have your ideas rejected? Accepted?
- How did this experience compare to real life?
- Why do we block other people's ideas?
- How can we increase our willingness and ability to accept ideas?

Source:
- Viola Spolin, Keith Johnstone, Fratelli Bologna, Theatresports

Character creation

Overview:
- As a group, the participants create a character, one feature or personality trait at a time. Beginning with a name, participants randomly take turns making offers until the character feels complete or the group loses a clear image of the character.

Improv topics:
- Spontaneity
- Listening and awareness
- Accepting offers
- Trust
- Storytelling
- Non-verbal behaviour

Purpose:
- Warm-up
- Team building
- Creativity
- Communication

Supplies:
- None

Time:
- 10–20 minutes

Number of players:
- 2–20

Game flow:
- Have the participants sit in a circle.
- Provide (or ask the group for) a fictional first and last name of a character (eg Sally McMurphy, Renaldo Hernandez, Clyde Clump, Isadora Ilandavalle).
- Have the participants randomly offer characteristics, building on the offers of others. (Example: 'Sally McMurphy is a waitress.' 'She has huge green eyes.' 'She moved to the United States from Ireland two years ago.' 'She moved because her family was really poor and she wanted to seek her fortune.')

- If someone in the group loses the picture of the character, because he or she feels an offer contradicts something that has already been said, or just doesn't make sense, that person can say, 'I can't see it', and the group will begin again with a new character.
- End work on a character when the group can no longer see it or feels the description is complete.
- Play as many rounds as you wish.

Variations:
- Have the group describe an environment (eg a hotel room, a haunted house, a train station, an office, a barn).
- Have the group describe a fictional product (eg Wiggy Wash, Yum-yum Paste, Ever-clean, Box-in-a-box).
- Have the group describe a character beginning with a characteristic other than a name (eg a profession, an age, a nationality, a physical characteristic).
- Have the group describe the future state of the team (see 'Vision weaving', page 186).

Tips:
- Encourage the group to speak up when they lose the vision of the character in the beginning. This allows the group to assess the kinds of risks they are willing to take, and to take a look at their assumptions.
- For use as an exercise on accepting offers, as the exercise progresses encourage the participants to expand their ability to 'see' characteristics that they were rejecting at first.
- Encourage the group to take their time.
- If a few members are dominating, ask for input from those who have not yet offered suggestions.
- This exercise can be used in diversity training to explore stereotypes. What characteristics do we associate with others? What are we unwilling to 'see'?

Suggested debrief questions:
- How did we work together? How aligned did you feel with the group vision?
- How did it feel to have your ideas accepted? Rejected?
- How did you censor yourself?
- What does this tell us about creating collaboratively?
- How do you feel about the people we created?
- What characteristics did we associate with others?

- Which characteristics did we see as incompatible?
- How does this translate to real interpersonal interactions?

Source:
- Adapted from Keith Johnstone

Circle mirror

Overview:
- Everyone stands in a circle and identifies someone across the circle to watch, so that each person is looking at a different member of the group. Then each person begins in a neutral position, and 'mirrors' or copies the other person's movements and facial expressions. No one attempts to initiate any movement.

Improv topics:
- Trust
- Listening and awareness
- Non-verbal behaviour

Purposes:
- Energy builder
- Team building
- Creativity
- Communication

Supplies:
- None

Time:
- 5–7 minutes

Number of players:
- 6–20

Game flow:
- Have the participants form a circle.
- One by one, have individuals choose someone across the circle to watch. This can be done by having the first person point to someone. The person pointed to puts a hand on his or her head to show he or she has been taken, and then points to someone else in turn until everyone has pointed and been pointed to once.
- Check the pattern by having everyone point to the person they are watching.
- Ask everyone to stand in a neutral position – feet shoulder-width apart, arms down at their sides, head straight.

- Tell everyone that they are not to initiate any movement intentionally, but that they should vigilantly mirror the person that they have chosen to watch.
- Start the game.

Variations:
- Play sitting in chairs.
- Play a more traditional mirror activity in which one person leads and everyone else follows.
- Begin with the traditional form and then, after a few moments, instruct the participants to initiate and follow collaboratively, without having any leader specified.

Tips:
- The results of this exercise will be that the group will start moving more and more – big gestures, facial expressions and movements – without anyone consciously initiating. This illustrates how many offers we make that we are unaware of.
- Double-check the pattern. If any of the links of people watching is broken, the exercise will not work.

Suggested debrief questions:
- What happened?
- Did anyone consciously initiate?
- Who assumed that someone had to be cheating?
- What does this mean?
- If we are making more offers than we are aware of, what are the ramifications?
- What does this tell us about communication?

Source:
- Adapted from Viola Spolin, Ruth Zapora, East Bay improv instructor, Patricia Ryan and Rebecca Stockley

Classic mirror

Overview:
- In pairs, participants 'mirror' each other – moving at the same time as if one were the other's reflection. The two take turns leading and following, and then finally attempt to move together with both leading and following at the same time.

Improv topics:
- Listening and awareness
- Trust
- Non-verbal behaviour

Purposes:
- Warm-up
- Team building
- Communication

Supplies:
- None

Time:
- 8–15 minutes

Number of players:
- Pairs

Game flow:
- Have the participants form pairs.
- Have the pairs face each other, and pick an A and a B.
- Assign Bs to be leaders and As to be followers. Explain that any movement that leaders make, followers will copy as if they are a mirror image. (If leaders move their right hand, followers will move their left as they face the leaders.)
- After a few minutes of Bs leading, instruct the pairs to switch leaders.
- After a few minutes of As leading, instruct the pairs to pass the lead back and forth at their own discretion until they themselves are unsure who is leading and who is following.
- Debrief.

Variations:
- Assign the pairs a specific activity (eg brushing their teeth).
- Play music in the background.
- Play as a group in a circle (see 'Circle mirror', page 132).

Tips:
- Ask the participants to play silently.
- Coach the participants to take care of their partners – if the follower can't keep up, it is the leader's responsibility to slow down.
- Remind the followers that they are responding as if they are a mirror reflection. Coach them individually, if need be.

Suggested debrief questions:
- Were you more comfortable leading or following?
- What happened as the exercise progressed?
- What kind of risks did you take?
- How did you limit yourself?
- How did it feel to communicate without words?
- What are the characteristics of a good leader?
- What are the characteristics of a good follower?

Source:
- Adapted from Viola Spolin

Conducted narrative

Overview:
- Four or five participants tell a story together, each person speaking when he or she is pointed to by a 'conductor'. Whenever the next person is pointed to, that person must continue exactly where the partner left off – even in the middle of a sentence or word.

Improv topics:
- Storytelling
- Listening and awareness
- Accepting offers
- Spontaneity

Purpose:
- Warm-up
- Team building
- Creativity
- Communication
- Review

Supplies:
- None

Time:
- 3–6 minutes per round

Number of players:
- 4–5 per round

Game flow:
- Ask for four or five volunteers.
- Tell the participants that they will tell a story.
- Explain that the person that you point to will talk. When you point to someone else, that person will continue wherever the previous person left off, even if it is in the middle of a sentence or a word.
- Get a suggested title for a never-before-told story from the observers and begin.
- Continue until the story is finished.

Variations:
- Assign two participants to be in charge of the action or plot and two to be in charge of the description. Participants must only describe or advance the action, based on their job.
- Play as an elimination game (see 'Elimination lists', page 142) in which participants who make mistakes are eliminated, and another participant from the large group takes the place of the eliminated person. In this case, mistakes include pausing too long before speaking, saying something that does not follow cleanly from the phrase or word before, and echoing (repeating) the last word that was said.
- Play simultaneously in sub-groups of four or five, with participants taking turns conducting each other.
- As a review activity, give the participants a process or concept to describe.
- Provide a genre or style of story. This version is good for inspiring people to think in different ways. It is also beneficial for exploring storytelling structures.

Tips:
- When conducting, make eye contact with the speakers and point with big, clear gestures.
- If the story gets completely muddled, begin a new one.
- Encourage the participants to be obvious and simple. With four people telling a story, there will be plenty of strangeness anyway.
- Have the participants tell the stories in the third person and past tense. That will allow action to take place and a consistent character voice to be maintained.
- See Chapter 6 for more general tips on storytelling skills.

Suggested debrief questions:
- What did you think of our stories?
- What was difficult? What was easy?
- How did you censor yourself?
- What made the story compelling?
- How was this different from telling a story yourself?
- What is the value of creating collaboratively?
- What are the pitfalls or frustrations?
- How does this relate to teamwork on the job?

Source:
- Adapted from Del Close's 'Conducted story', Chicago City Limits and Theatresports

Conversation weave

Overview:
- Three or four participants tell stories as if they are talking to a friend. The individuals speak a few sentences at a time and then let someone else speak. The stories are unrelated, but the participants weave details and words from the other stories into their own.

Improv topics:
- Listening and awareness
- Accepting offers
- Storytelling

Purpose:
- Team building
- Creativity
- Communication

Supplies:
- None

Time:
- 8–15 minutes per group

Number of players:
- 3–4 per group

Game flow:
- Three or four volunteers stand in front of the group.
- Assign a topic or theme.
- One of the participants starts to tell a story. After a few sentences, the first participant stops and a second participant starts his or her story. Then the next person starts.
- After the stories have been established, the individuals take turns to randomly offer new parts of their stories a few sentences at a time.
- As they continue with their stories, the participants weave words from the other stories into their own.

Variations:
- Conduct the participants by pointing to them or calling out the name of the next person to speak.

- Have the participants act as if they are speaking on the phone and have them weave the other conversations into theirs.
- Have three pairs of participants role-play conversations and weave in words from the other conversations.

Tips:
- Encourage the participants to weave in the words without letting their stories become the same.
- Coach (or conduct) the participants to increase the speed with which they switch speakers as the exercise advances.

Suggested debrief questions:
- Observers, what did you notice? What was compelling about this activity?
- Storytellers, which words or phrases stood out to you?
- Did this activity make the storytelling easier or more difficult?
- How does this activity relate to real life?
- How can we use this ability to increase creativity and communication?

Source:
- Adapted from Del Close's 'Cocktail party' and Chicago improv schools' 'Telephone bank'

Declare yourself

Overview:
- The participants stand in a circle. One by one, they step forward into the centre of the circle, make eye contact with the other members and say, 'I am [name] and I am here.'

Improv topics:
- Trust
- Listening and awareness
- Non-verbal behaviour

Purpose:
- Ice-breaker
- Warm-up
- Team building
- Communication
- Needs assessment
- Review
- Closing

Supplies:
- None

Time:
- 5–15 minutes

Number of players:
- 3–20

Game flow:
- Have the participants stand in a circle.
- One at a time, as they feel the impulse to, each participant takes a step toward the centre of the circle.
- First the person who has stepped forward looks around the circle, making eye contact with the other participants.
- Then the person says, 'I am [name] and I am here.'
- After a moment, he or she steps back and someone else steps forward.

Variations:
- Have the participants state their intention for a meeting or workshop (eg 'I intend to improve my ability to give effective feedback'). This is an effective needs assessment activity.

- Have the participants step forward and make eye contact with everyone in silence.
- End a workshop by having participants share one thing that they learnt in the session.

Tips:
- Encourage the participants to take their time.
- There should be no talking other than the words of the person stepping forward.
- In its pure form, this activity is surprisingly powerful. Make sure you create a safe space for potential vulnerability.

Suggested debrief questions:
- How did this feel?
- What surprised you?
- What was the most difficult part?
- What does this tell you about giving a presentation? About communication in general?
- How do you feel as a team now?

Source:
- Adapted from Patricia Ryan's 'I am here'

Elimination lists

Overview:
- Four or five participants stand in front of the group. The facilitator assigns a category (or gets one from the group) and points to individual participants. Each participant must name something that fits into that category (eg category – breakfast cereals, participants – 'Cheerios', 'corn flakes', 'porridge'). If participants make a mistake, they are eliminated and another person takes their place.

Improv topics:
- Spontaneity
- Listening and awareness
- Trust

Purpose:
- Ice-breaker
- Warm-up
- Energy builder
- Team building
- Creativity
- Communication
- Review

Supplies:
- None

Time:
- 6–12 minutes

Number of players:
- 4–20 (or more with increased time, or if some behave as observers only)

Game flow:
- Ask for four or five volunteers.
- Instruct them that you will get a category from the observers. When you point to each participant you want that person to name something that fits into the category.
- If the person makes a mistake, it is the job of the observers to make a buzzer sound and the person will be eliminated.
- Explain that a mistake consists of one of three things: pausing too long

before saying something, saying something that has already been said and saying something that does not fit into the category.
- Ask the remaining participants for a category and begin.
- Each time someone is eliminated, get a new volunteer to take the person's place, and a new category.
- Continue the activity, ideally, until all participants have had the chance to play.

Variations:
- As a review activity, assign the topic yourself.
- Play with the entire group at the same time, eliminating people until you have one grand prizewinner.
- Have participants take turns conducting the activity.

Tips:
- This activity is useful for discussing the value of failing gracefully. Encourage the participants to take a big bow when they make a mistake.
- Increase the speed as the activity continues.
- Use clear, big gestures and make eye contact with the participants while conducting.

Suggested debrief questions:
- Why was that fun?
- How did you feel when you made a mistake?
- How did you feel when someone else made a mistake?
- What helped you do well at this activity?
- Why is it so hard to think of something to say, when there are so many choices?
- How would we get better at this?
- What happened as the activity continued? Did you want to play more or less?
- What does this have to do with creativity and teamwork?

Source:
- Adapted from Del Close's 'Conducted story' and Theatresports

Emotional meeting

Overview:
- Four people role-play having a meeting. They enter the room one at a time with a different emotional attitude. Each time a new person in the room enters, everyone takes on that person's emotion. When the individuals leave, in reverse order, the remaining people revert to the previous emotion.

Improv topics:
- Trust
- Spontaneity
- Accepting offers
- Listening and awareness
- Non-verbal behaviour

Purposes:
- Energy builder
- Team building
- Communication

Supplies:
- Chairs and table (optional)
- Flip chart and markers (optional)

Time:
- 5–10 minutes per group

Number of players:
- 3–5 per group

Game flow:
- Ask for three to five volunteers.
- Tell them that they are going to role-play a meeting. One by one, they will enter, and then leave over the course of about five minutes.
- Assign each individual an emotion or attitude. (You can field them from the rest of the group. Get a variety, eg joy, anger, fear and ambition.)
- Assign an order for the individuals to enter the playing area, and review all the emotions.
- Let the group know that whenever a new person enters, they are all to take on that emotion.

- Then explain that after the last person has been in the room for a while, he or she will leave and everyone will revert to the previous emotion, until the next person leaves, and so on till the last person is left with his or her original emotion.
- Run the activity.

Variations:
- Play 'Emotional car pool' in which the members are in a car, picking up individuals on their way to work and then dropping them off.
- Play in gibberish.
- Play silently.

Tips:
- Gather disparate emotions for each round.
- Be prepared to coach from the side as the activity progresses. Remind people what the current emotion is, if they forget, and prompt people to enter or leave.
- Expect raucous fun.

Suggested debrief questions:
- Why was this fun?
- How does this experience mirror real meetings?
- What effect does taking on others' feelings have?
- How can we use this effect for good?
- Can we control our emotions? How? Do we want to? Why?
- Which emotions served the meeting best?

Source:
- Adapted from the Chicago schools, Freestyle Repertory Theatre, Theatresports

Gibberish press conference

Overview:
- One player speaks in a nonsense language, as if they were a foreign leader at a press conference. Another player translates the 'gibberish' into English.

Improv topics:
- Spontaneity
- Accepting offers
- Storytelling
- Non-verbal behaviours

Purpose:
- Energy builder
- Team building
- Creativity
- Communication
- Review

Supplies:
- None

Time:
- 5–30 minutes

Number of players:
- Pairs

Game flow:
- Explain the concept of gibberish and demonstrate it.
- Have participants turn to a partner and say something in gibberish.
- Ask for two volunteers.
- Give the pair a topic, or have the other workshop participants provide one.
- Have one of the players speak in gibberish and the other translate.
- Allow the other participants to ask questions, which can be translated into gibberish by the interpreter.

Variations:
- Set up a talk show with a foreign guest, an interpreter and a host who speaks English. The interpreter translates both the gibberish and the English.

- For presentation skills training, have participants practise their presentations completely in gibberish.
- Play gibberish poet, in which the interpreter translates a poem.
- Have a participant who speaks a foreign language that the group is not familiar with use his or her native tongue rather than gibberish.
- In a circle, have the participants take turns translating a line of gibberish and then adding a line of their own that is translated by the next person. This can be done as a continuous story or as unrelated phrases. (This activity can also be used as a warm-up activity for the other versions.)
- Dictate a story in gibberish, one line at a time. Have the participants write down their translations of your sentences as you go. Ask individuals to share their translations at the end.

Tips:
- Be gentle. When people are asked to make up nonsense, they can feel silly. Do not underestimate the risk you are asking certain individuals to take.
- Gibberish can be anything. If participants are resistant, coach them to say, 'blah, blah, blah'.
- Be willing to demonstrate gibberish to encourage others.
- Remind participants that whatever they say in English or in gibberish is right.
- Coach participants to say 'Yes' when asked a question.

Suggested debrief questions:
- How did it feel to communicate without words?
- What communication cues do we have other than words?
- Observers, did the translation match the interpretations you made in your heads?
- How did it feel to accept offers?
- How did it feel to have your offers accepted?
- What happens when we say 'Yes' as opposed to 'No'?
- In what ways did you censor yourself? Translators? Gibberish speakers?

Source:
- Adapted from Viola Spolin, the Chicago improv community, Freestyle Repertory Theatre and Theatresports

Giving gifts

Overview:
- In pairs, participants exchange imaginary gifts. One person hands the other an imaginary object. That person says, 'Oh, it's a —. Thanks!' Then the second person gives another gift to the first person. The participants continue to give and receive gifts back and forth for the duration of the activity.

Improv topics:
- Accepting offers
- Spontaneity
- Trust
- Non-verbal behaviour

Purpose:
- Ice-breaker
- Warm-up
- Team building
- Creativity
- Communication

Supplies:
- None

Time:
- 5–15 minutes

Number of players:
- Pairs

Game flow:
- Divide the participants into pairs.
- Have the participants choose an A and a B.
- A presents B with an imaginary gift.
- B accepts and identifies the gift, saying, 'Oh, it's a —. Thank you! I love it.'
- Then B gives A a gift, and so on.

Variations:
- Play silently.
- Play in a circle.

Tips:
- Explain that participants may be very specific with their physical indications or more general. (For example, the giver may mime unclasping a necklace or reading a book, and then hand the object over. Or she might just put out her hands and offer up some nondescript object.)
- Remind the participants to accept the offer enthusiastically. Part of the exercise is arbitrary positive acceptance.
- Remind the participants that it is the receiver who ultimately defines the gift. If the giver unclasps what she thinks is a necklace and hands it over, and the receiver says, 'Oh, it's a boa constrictor!', then the object becomes a snake.
- Encourage the participants to go fast.
- Play for long enough for the participants to exhaust their initial thoughts and move on to spontaneous invention.

Suggested debrief questions:
- How did it feel to receive the gifts?
- What was your experience of having to identify the gift?
- How did if feel to give gifts?
- What happened when your gift was identified as something other than what you intended?
- Which felt more comfortable, giving or receiving?
- How did the exercise change as it continued?
- What was your experience of having to accept the gifts with enthusiasm?
- How does this activity relate to real life?

Source:
- Viola Spolin, Keith Johnstone and Freestyle Repertory Theatre

Hum circle

Overview:
- The participants stand in a circle and, with their eyes closed, make sounds, creating harmonies and musical patterns.

Improv topics:
- Spontaneity
- Accepting offers
- Listening and awareness
- Trust

Purpose:
- Warm-up
- Team building
- Communication
- Closing

Supplies:
- None

Time:
- 5–10 minutes

Number of players:
- 4–16 people

Game flow:
- Have the participants stand in a circle with their shoulders touching.
- Instruct them to close their eyes, or focus on the centre of the circle if they are more comfortable.
- Have them begin to hum as they feel the impulse. Each participant should listen to the others and contribute in response.
- Continue until the group discovers a natural ending.

Variations:
- Give the group a theme around which to create (eg winter, productivity, teamwork).
- Have the participants make all sorts of sounds in addition to humming.
- Give the participants simple musical instruments, like triangles, drums or maracas.

- Have the participants sit in chairs, in groups of four, and make music by humming or playing instruments.

Tips:
- Encourage the participants to take their time.
- Encourage them to make offers in response to other sounds.
- This activity can be a nice way to end a session.

Suggested debrief questions:
- How spontaneous did you feel?
- Which moments do you remember?
- What kind of stories did you make up in your head?
- What kinds of emotions were elicited?
- How does this experience inform our work as a team?

Source:
- General acting training

Idea circle

Overview:
- The participants stand in a circle. The group passes an object (eg a ball, a stick or a shoe) around the circle, while one of the participants names all the words he or she can that begin with a specific letter. When the object gets around the circle to that participant, the participant stops and gives a new letter to the next person.

Improv topic:
- Spontaneity

Purpose:
- Warm-up
- Energy builder
- Creativity
- Review

Supplies:
- One object

Time:
- 20–30 seconds per participant per round

Number of players:
- 10–20

Game flow:
- Have the participants stand in a circle.
- Give the first participant an object that the group can pass around the circle (eg a ball, a stuffed animal, a juggling pin).
- Ask the participant to give the object to the person on his or her left, and a letter of the alphabet to the person on the right.
- The person on the right then begins to name words that begin with that letter while the group passes the object around the circle.
- As soon as the object gets to the person who is speaking, that person stops.
- Then he or she offers a letter to the person on the right and passes the object to the left. This continues till everyone has had a chance.

Variations:
- Have the participants brainstorm ideas around a specific topic (eg ways to make meetings more effective or ways to cut costs).
- Have the participants name the steps of a process as review.
- Have the participants name customer characteristics or needs.
- Have the participants list their individual job responsibilities as a getting-to-know-each-other exercise.

Tips:
- Encourage the participants to keep talking, even if they repeat themselves or say something that doesn't make sense.
- Encourage the group to pass the object quickly, especially if it is a large group.
- This activity lends itself to any topic that can involve listing words or characteristics.

Suggested debrief questions:
- How do you feel compared to when we started?
- How did you censor yourself?
- Why was this energizing?
- What is the value of passing the object?

Source:
- Chicago City Limits

Neutral status scene

Overview:
- Participants are given a short script of 8–10 lines of neutral dialogue. The scene may be completely neutral, or depict a job interview or coaching session (see the sample scene below). Pairs take turns enacting the scene, playing with the status relationships through their non-verbal choices. The rest of the group observes.

Improv topics:
- Non-verbal behaviour
- Listening and awareness
- Storytelling

Purpose:
- Team building
- Communication

Supplies:
- Handouts, flip chart or slide with the scene recorded

Time:
- 15–30 minutes

Number of players:
- Pairs

Game flow:
- Give out handouts of the scene or display it on flip chart or slide.
- Recruit two volunteers to act it out.
- Allow the participants to play the scene once without any outside direction.
- Discuss the perceived status of each character.
- Assign status roles to each player and have them play the scene again. Combinations can include:
  - Person A is high; Person B is low.
  - Person B is high; Person A is low.
  - Both are high.
  - Both are low.
  - Status remains equal but shifts.
  - Status switches: one starts high and ends low; the other starts low and ends high.
- Substitute the two players with others and continue to try different combinations.
- Discuss as you go.

- Debrief.

Variations:
- Use one pair to demonstrate and then divide participants into trios to practise – two actors and one observer.
- Have the group write their own neutral scene.
- Set up status battles where the observers vote on who is the lowest or the highest.
- Add 30 seconds of silence somewhere in the scene.
- Allow teams to improvise scenes in their own words.

Tips:
- Sample scene: the job interview
  A: *Good morning.*
  B: Good morning.
  A: *Have a seat.*
  B: Thank you.
  A: *I have looked over your CV.*
  B: Yes?
  A: *I see you worked at Global Limited.*
  B: Yes. For a number of years.
  A: *Very impressive.*
  B: Thanks.
- If you have the participants create the scene, make sure the dialogue really feels neutral.
- Allow one team to try a couple of different status interactions before moving on to the next team.
- Feel free to freeze the action of the scene in the middle to point out an especially clear status moment.
- Be aware that attempts to claim status can backfire. High-status people can fall quickly if the other person fails to be intimidated, and low-status people can gain status by being too self-focused.

Suggested debrief questions:
- How much do you think the words mattered in this interaction?
- What were the most effective ways to raise your status?
- What lowered status?
- What status choices would you like to make in a real-life interview? A sales call? A coaching session?
- What is the value of being aware of status behaviour in general?

Source:
- Adapted from Keith Johnstone's *Impro* (1979) and Freestyle Repertory Theatre

One-sided scene

Overview:
- Two participants role-play an interaction. One of them can speak. The other may only respond non-verbally.

Improv topics:
- Non-verbal behaviour
- Listening and awareness
- Accepting offers

Purpose:
- Team building
- Communication

Supplies:
- None

Time:
- 3–5 minutes per role-play

Number of players:
- Pairs

Game flow:
- Ask for two volunteers.
- Assign a scenario (eg a job interview, a coaching session, an interview with a reporter, a father and son driving home from school, etc) and an objective or goal for one of the participants.
- Allow that participant to speak. The other must react and respond naturally, but without using any words.
- Role-play the interaction until the objective is achieved or until time runs out.

Variations:
- Play half the scenario with one person speaking and then switch in the middle.
- Call out which person may speak and switch back and forth at various intervals.
- Play in concurrent groups with two participants and one or two observers in each group.

- Role-play the scenario completely silently, with neither participant speaking.
- Allow the non-speaking participant to have two or three words that he or she can repeat (eg 'Yes', 'Certainly', 'I thought so', 'Is that right?').

Tips:
- Coach non-speaking participants to act as naturally as possible, finding some justification for not speaking. Remind them not to mime or exaggerate their behaviour as in charades.
- Coach speakers to notice and accept the offers that their partners are making. Are they giving in? Are they objecting? Have they agreed?
- The objectives or goals should involve the other person (eg 'Get her to give me the job', 'Convince him to come to work on time', 'Let my son know I'm getting a divorce without having him hate me').

Suggested debrief questions:
- What kind of signals did you get from your partner's non-verbal behaviour?
- How easy was it to read your partner's reactions?
- When did you find yourself paying attention to your partner's facial expressions and body? When did you ignore them?
- Non-speakers, how involved did you feel? How much of an effect did you feel you were able to have?
- Observers, how easy was it for you to read the non-speakers?
- How did you feel when you saw something that the speaker did not seem to respond to?
- Speakers, did you know when you had met your objective?
- What did you do when you felt your tactics weren't working?
- How can we use this type of awareness in real life?

Source:
- Adapted from Chicago City Limits

One-word-at-a-time exercises

Overview:
- A variety of foundational exercises that is ubiquitous in the improv community. A number of participants narrate a story or answer questions, each contributing only one word each turn.

Improv topics:
- Spontaneity
- Accepting offers
- Listening and awareness
- Storytelling

Purpose:
- Warm-up
- Energy builder
- Team building
- Creativity
- Communication
- Review

Supplies:
- None

Time:
- 5–30 minutes

Number of players:
- 2–20

Game flow:
- Have participants stand in a circle.
- Provide a topic or title for a story.
- Tell the story with each successive person contributing the next word.

Variations:
- Tell a story two words at a time.
- Tell a story with each person adding one word the first time around the circle, then two words, then three and then four in successive passes around the circle. Then go back down: three words, two and finally one, ending the story when it is the last person's turn to say one word.

- Tell a word-at-a-time story in pairs.
- Tell a word-at-a-time story in pairs, acting out the action of the story as you go.
- Create a word-at-a-time talk show on which a host interviews a word-at-a-time expert (see page 55).
- Create word-at-a-time 'proverbs' that summarize the learning of the day. (One way to do this is to give each person in the circle only one turn, so that the proverb must end with the last person.)

Tips:
- Remind the participants that there is no such thing as a small word; 'a' and 'the' are as necessary to the sense of the sentence as 'sledge' or 'restructuring'.
- Participants can end a sentence with the inflection of their voice.
- Encourage eye contact.
- Encourage speed.

Suggested debrief questions:
- When did you feel satisfied? When were you frustrated?
- Did you censor yourself? How?
- Why did I encourage us to go quickly?
- What would happen if we did this every day for a year?
- How is this like teamwork on the job?

Source:
- Viola Spolin, Keith Johnstone, Chicago schools, Theatresports

Paired drawing

Overview:
- In pairs, participants draw a face or other picture, alternating one line or feature at a time. Then they give it a title one letter at a time (see page 58 for examples).

Improv topics:
- Spontaneity
- Accepting offers
- Non-verbal behaviour

Purpose:
- Team building
- Creativity
- Communication

Supplies:
- Coloured pens, and paper or flip chart

Time:
- 10–20 minutes

Number of players:
- Pairs

Game flow:
- Distribute pens and paper.
- Explain that the task will be for each pair to draw a face, alternating one line or feature at a time.
- As soon as someone hesitates, the drawing is finished.
- Then the pair will give the drawing a title, alternating letters until one person hesitates.
- Ask for a volunteer and model the activity.
- Allow the pairs to draw a few faces, or move on to another picture that they wish to draw.
- Display the results.
- Debrief the process and the products.

Variations:
- Leave the subject of the drawing open.

- Pass the drawings around a circle or in groups of three to five participants.
- Have the entire group create a mural.

Suggested debrief questions:
- How was that process?
- Were there any moments when you censored yourself?
- Were there any moments when you objected to your partner's offer?
- What do you think of the results?
- How do these pictures compare to the drawings you think we would have created individually?
- What are the advantages to collaboration?
- What are the disadvantages?
- How is this like the kinds of teamwork you experience on the job?

Source:
- Originally taken from Johnstone's 'Eyes' exercise, with adaptations by Creative Advantage, Dan Klein, Bay Area Theatresports and Fratelli Bologna

Picture maths

Overview:
- Participants work in groups of three. The person in the middle is in the 'hot seat'. The participant on that person's right asks the person to describe imaginary pictures in a photo album. The third participant intersperses simple maths problems for the participant in the 'hot seat' to solve at the same time.

Improv topics:
- Spontaneity
- Accepting offers
- Listening and awareness
- Storytelling

Purpose:
- Warm-up
- Energy builder
- Creativity

Supplies:
- None

Time:
- 10–15 minutes

Number of players:
- 3 per group

Game flow:
- Split the participants into triads. (If there are leftover people, create groups of four with one observer for each round.)
- Ask them to stand in a horseshoe.
- The person in the middle is in the 'hot seat', and opens an imaginary picture album.
- The participant on that person's right is in charge of asking the person to describe the pictures in the album (eg 'Who is that?' 'What is she wearing?' 'Where is that place?' 'What is that painting in the background?').
- The participant on the person's left periodically asks *simple* addition and subtraction problems while this is going on, using the previous answer as the first number of the next problem (eg '3 plus 3'... 'minus 2'...

'plus 10'). This requires the middle player to do both maths and remember the previous number.

- After a few minutes the participants switch, until each person has played each role.

Variations:
- Ask the participant on the right to interview the person rather than ask the person to describe pictures.
- Ask the person to describe the pictures in rhyme.

Tips:
- Model the activity before it begins.
- Coach the individuals asking questions not to provide too much information (eg ask 'Who is that?' not 'Who is that woman with the blue wig sitting in the rocking chair?').
- Coach the people asking questions to switch the topic or turn the page if the 'hot seat' person seems to be getting too comfortable.
- Remind the individuals asking the maths problems to keep them simple. The activity is difficult enough.
- The maths problems should be asked at intervals that keep the 'hot seat' person on his or her toes, but allow some time to focus on the imaginary pictures.
- Coach the person in the middle to keep talking until interrupted with a maths problem and then go right back to describing the picture.
- Coach the person to say a number quickly and move on, even if he or she is not sure that it is right.

Suggested debrief questions:
- What do you think is going on in this exercise? (We are working our conscious rational mind to distract it from interfering with our creative impulses. We are also stimulating our brains visually, orally, aurally, artistically and rationally all at the same time. This game is a virtual brain gym.)
- How many found it harder to do the maths? How many found it harder to describe the pictures?
- Did your descriptions surprise you?
- What did you notice while you were asking questions? Maths problems?
- What images do you remember?

Source:
- Adapted from Chicago City Limits

Picture poetry

Overview:
- In pairs, participants describe an imaginary picture in verse.

Improv topics:
- Spontaneity
- Accepting offers
- Listening and awareness
- Storytelling

Purpose:
- Warm-up
- Team building
- Creativity
- Communication

Supplies:
- None

Time:
- 4–10 minutes

Number of players:
- Pairs

Game flow:
- Divide the participants into pairs.
- Ask for one pair to volunteer to demonstrate.
- Instruct the two participants to imagine that they are viewing a picture in a gallery.
- Have the first person offer a sentence describing the picture.
- Have the second person offer a second sentence that rhymes with the first. Then have the second person offer a third line.
- The first person rhymes with that line and offers another that does not rhyme, and so forth.
- Continue for two minutes or until the picture seems complete.
- Have the rest of the participants engage in the activity simultaneously.

Variations:
- Have the participants describe the picture without rhyming.
- Play with three to five participants.
- Have the participants tell a story or describe an event in rhyme.

Tips:
- Rhyming is easier than it seems. If the participants are nervous, you can warm them up by shouting out a word and having the entire group shout back a rhyming word simultaneously. You may also coach participants to say a nonsense word if they cannot think of an actual word that rhymes.
- Coach the participants to go fast, so that they do not fall victim to their censors.
- Provide a suggestion for the type of picture the pairs are looking at if they feel stuck.

Suggested debrief questions:
- How did it feel to rhyme?
- What kind of picture did you describe?
- What surprised you about what you created?
- How well did you work together?
- What was difficult? What was easy?
- What is the value of rhyming? (We make offers to ourselves when we rhyme. Being forced to come up with a rhyme prompts us to think outside the box, as well as to do more than one thing at the same time – a great way to bypass our censors.)

Source:
- Michael Gelman, the Chicago improv schools

Safety zone

Overview:
- Participants secretly pick enemies and bodyguards, and attempt to keep their bodyguards between them and their enemies.

Improv topics:
- Spontaneity
- Accepting offers
- Non-verbal behaviour

Purpose:
- Warm-up
- Energy builder
- Team building

Supplies:
- None

Time:
- 3–6 minutes

Number of players:
- 8–100

Game flow:
- Ask each participant to look around the room and privately decide on one other person to be Person A.
- Then ask each participant to pick another person, again secretly, to be Person B.
- Inform participants that Person A is their enemy and Person B is their bodyguard. The goal is to make sure that your bodyguard is between you and your enemy at all times.
- Before people start to move, remind them to walk and that no one should get hurt.
- Play two or three rounds, choosing new enemies and bodyguards each time.

Variations:
- Call the game 'Eclipse' and use the words 'sun' and 'moon' rather than 'enemy' and 'bodyguard'.

- As a final round, make each person play the role of bodyguard, so that Person A remains the enemy but Person B becomes the person to be protected. The job of the participants, then, is to stay in between A and B.

Tips:
- The process will result in a wild, swirling pattern. Continue to remind people to walk. This activity is significantly more fun than it appears on paper.
- The last variation will result in a tight clump of people.
- Check for physical limitations before playing the game, and remind people to *walk* not run.

Suggested debrief questions:
- What happened?
- How do you feel? Why are you laughing?
- What feels different now?
- What is the value of physical activity?

Source:
- Theatresports, Freestyle Repertory Theatre and Diane Rachel

Slap pass

Overview:
- The participants stand in a circle. Someone claps hands in the direction of someone else. That person passes the clap along to someone else, and so forth. The game should go very quickly.

Improv topics:
- Spontaneity
- Listening and awareness
- Accepting offers
- Trust
- Non-verbal behaviour
- Storytelling

Purpose:
- Warm-up
- Energy builder
- Team building
- Creativity
- Communication

Supplies:
- None

Time:
- 5–15 minutes

Number of players:
- 5–25

Game flow:
- Have the participants stand in a circle.
- One person claps at another, making eye contact and pointing hands in the other person's direction.
- That person claps at the next person, and so on, randomly around the circle.

Variations:
- Participants clap in order around the circle, gradually speeding up until the slap is going around the circle as fast as possible.

- Participants pass the clap around the circle, clapping in pairs simultaneously. Person A and Person B clap together, then B and C, then C and D and so forth. The goal is to increase the speed and, at the same time, clap exactly in unison.
- Participants clap around the circle, but can change direction whenever they wish, passing the clap back around the other way. This is a good game for discussing patterns (see Chapter 6).
- Participants clap around the circle and can change directions. When they are clapping to the right, they clap once. When they are clapping to the left they clap twice.

Tips:
- The original version of the game is a wonderful warm-up, energy generator and spontaneity exercise.
- The other more complicated versions are good for beginning discussions on storytelling, specifically pattern creation and reincorporation. After teaching the game, coach participants to look for patterns and try to repeat them. You may also ask a group to tell a story with claps.
- In the versions of the game that permit changing direction, you may tell the group that changing direction is making a new offer. Continuing in the same direction is accepting an offer. Debrief the effect of each choice.
- Coach participants must not talk during the exercise.
- Coach participants must make their partners look good – no looking at one person and clapping at another.

Suggested debrief questions:
- What kinds of stories did you make up, based on the clap patterns?
- What helped you go faster?
- How do you feel compared to when we began?
- How does this relate to collaboration and communication in the workplace?

Source:
- Theatresports

Speech tag

Overview:
- In groups of three or four, participants tell a story, tagging each other when they want to take over the narrative.

Improv topics:
- Spontaneity
- Accepting offers
- Listening and awareness
- Storytelling
- Non-verbal behaviour

Purpose:
- Team building
- Creativity
- Communication
- Review

Supplies:
- None

Time:
- 3–5 minutes per group

Number of players:
- 3–5 per group

Game flow:
- Ask for three to five volunteers.
- Have one person stand in front with the others behind in a horseshoe.
- Give the group a suggestion of something to talk about – a story title, a character or product name, a technical process.
- Have the person in front begin to talk. After a bit, have the second person tag the first person out (tap him or her on the shoulder) and continue the story exactly where the first person left off.
- Have the other participants randomly tag in and continue the story until it is finished, all the participants tagging in when they feel they want to or when their partner needs to be relieved.
- Continue until the story is done.

Variations:
- Have the players take over in order.
- Have each player tag in only once, ending the story with the last player.
- Have the players speak in rhyme.
- Have the players tell the story as a monologue, taking on the same character body and voice. (This version is especially good for non-verbal behaviour discussions.)
- Instruct the players when to switch, calling out their names or pointing to them (see 'Conducted narrative', page 136).

Tips:
- Coach the players to tag in even if they do not know what they are going to say, especially if their partner seems to need help.
- Coach the players to increase the speed with which they tag in.
- Coach the players to start speaking exactly where their partner left off.

Suggested debrief questions:
- When did you choose to jump in?
- When did you hesitate?
- What was difficult? What was enjoyable?
- What kind of offers were there to accept?
- What were you thinking about while you were not speaking?
- How do you feel about what you created as a group?

Source:
- Freestyle Repertory Theatre, Chicago improv schools

Spontaneous marketing

Overview:
- In groups, participants brainstorm a name, logo, tag line and ad campaign.

Improv topics:
- Spontaneity
- Accepting offers

Purpose:
- Ice-breaker
- Team building
- Creativity
- Communication

Supplies:
- Flip charts (one per group)
- Markers

Time:
- 15–20 minutes plus 3 minutes per group to share

Number of players:
- 2–5 per group

Game flow:
- Divide the participants into equal groups of two to five participants, and provide each one with a flip chart and markers.
- Tell them that they have 12 minutes to come up with the following for marketing themselves as a group:
  - a name;
  - a logo;
  - a tag line;
  - an ad campaign (eg a TV commercial that shows…, a billboard that says…).
- At three-minute intervals remind them to move on to the next topic if they haven't already done so.
- Require that every member of the group be involved in the presentation of the results.
- Have each group present its 'pitch'.

Variations:
- Have each group pitch a topic or product from the training.
- Have each group improvise their pitch – each participant throws out an idea and the rest of the group builds on it without planning.
- Have groups create a poem or song that describes their group.
- Have groups create a secret handshake.

Tips:
- Enforcing shortish time limits helps the creative process. If people feel that they did not have enough time, that does two things: gives them an excuse not to be brilliant, and honours their spontaneous responses without over-evaluating.
- Walk around as the groups are working and encourage them to accept ideas.
- You may wish to run the activity as a contest, and judge on creativity and participation. If you do, it is possible to have the results be a tie, or to have prizes for each team. The pay-off of framing the activity as a contest may be increased motivation. The price for having one winner may be a reduced level of comfort in being spontaneous or creative.

Suggested debrief questions:
- How did the process go in your individual groups?
- Were there things that would have made you feel more comfortable or successful as individuals? How about as a team?
- What did you especially enjoy?
- How do you feel about the results?
- How would they have been different if you had been working alone?
- What is the value of collaboration as against individual creativity?
- What did you learn about the creative process?

Source:
- Adapted from Viola Spolin and Del Close's 'Ad game'

Status demo

Overview:
- Participants mingle, as if at a party, with half of the group displaying high-status physical behaviours and the other half low-status behaviours. After a few minutes, the groups switch.

Improv topics:
- Trust
- Non-verbal behaviours
- Listening and awareness

Purpose:
- Warm-up
- Team building
- Communication

Supplies:
- None

Time:
- 5–15 minutes

Number of players:
- 5–100

Game flow:
- Split the group in two.
- Assign one group to take on the following high-status behaviours:
    - Take up as much space in the room as possible, physically and vocally.
    - Move smoothly.
    - Make eye contact and hold it comfortably.
    - Make (appropriate) physical contact directly and comfortably.
    - Hold your head still, but not stiff.
- Assign the other group to take on low-status behaviours:
    - Take up as little space as possible.
    - Say 'um' and 'ah' when you talk.
    - Touch your face and hair often.
    - Try to make eye contact, but find it a bit painful.
    - Want to make physical contact, but find it difficult.

- Tell the two groups that they are at a party. They all know each other and are happy to be there. Have the groups mingle. Inform them that they may talk to anyone they wish, from either group.
- After a few minutes, have the participants switch status roles. Remind the group of the specific behaviours and have them mingle again.
- Debrief.

Variations:
- Do not tell the group that you are focusing on status. See what assumptions they make about the members of the other group.
- Assign just one behaviour to each group and see how it informs the rest of their behaviours.
- If there are few enough participants, have them interact as if they were in a meeting.
- First have everyone take on high-status behaviours, and then low, before mixing the two.

Tips:
- Status is touchy. Leave time for discussion.
- 'Status pass', 'Status cards' and 'Neutral status scene' are potential follow-up exercises. Each of them explores status in subtler ways than this activity.

Suggested debrief questions:
- How did you feel in each role?
- Was one more comfortable than the other?
- What assumptions did you make about the other people?
- Whom were you more comfortable talking to?
- What happens to communication as the status gap grows?
- How much does our physicality affect status in real life?
- How else is this exercise a reflection of the real world?
- What are some examples of status interactions in your jobs?

Source:
- Keith Johnstone, Bay Area Theatresports, Fratelli Bologna

Status pass

Overview:
- The participants stand in a circle, and take turns verbally or non-verbally lowering and then raising the status of the person to their right.

Improv topics:
- Trust
- Non-verbal behaviour

Purpose:
- Warm-up
- Team building
- Communication

Supplies:
- None

Time:
- 5–15 minutes

Number of players:
- 2–20 per group

Game flow:
- Have participants stand in a circle.
- Instruct the first person to turn to his or her right and lower the status of the next person with a phrase or gesture.
- That person does the same, and so on around the circle.
- Then have the first person raise the next person's status, and continue through the rest of the group.

Variations:
- Raise and lower status with non-verbal behaviour only.
- Play in pairs trading back and forth.
- Assign a neutral line of dialogue to each participant.
- Instruct the participants to decide privately whether they wish to raise or lower their partner's status and then have the rest of the group guess their intention.

Tips:
- It is important to lower status first and then raise it, so that participants are left feeling validated, not dismissed.
- 'Status cards' and 'Neutral status scene' are potential follow-up activities.

Source:
- Adapted from Keith Johnstone and Chicago City Limits

Story seeds

Overview:
- The facilitator or group members come up with four neutral sentences. Then, individually, they write stories encompassing those four sentences, but adding characterizations and details.

Improv topics:
- Storytelling
- Accepting offers

Purpose:
- Creativity
- Communication
- Needs assessment
- Problem solving
- Review

Supplies:
- Pens and paper

Time:
- 10–20 minutes

Number of players:
- Variable

Game flow:
- The facilitator presents four neutral sentences or elicits them from the group. (Example: The manager walked into the call centre. The lights flickered. Joe ate a sandwich. The computer froze.)
- Each individual writes a story or monologue incorporating those four sentences however they wish to.
- Give the participants approximately 10 minutes to write their stories.
- Share as desired.

Variations:
- As a review activity provide content words or models, rather than sentences.
- As a problem-solving exercise, provide an objective in addition to the four sentences.

- Allow participants to work in pairs or teams.
- Provide a first and last sentence only.

Tips:
- Some individuals are comfortable writing and working alone. Others are not. This activity can balance more collaborative and public activities.
- Do not force anyone to share what they have written.
- Give the participants the leeway to interpret the assignment however they wish. If they want to write a memo or dialogue, for example, let them. If they find themselves writing four separate small pieces, encourage them to follow their creative impulses.

Suggested debrief questions:
- What inspired you?
- How did you censor yourself?
- What did you especially enjoy in the stories you heard?
- What made these stories compelling?
- How could you use the process of writing to help you in other ways?

Source:
- Adapted from Kenn Adams and Freestyle Repertory Theatre

Story visioning

Overview:
- Using the story spine (see below), participants assume that their ideal vision of the future is the happy ending of a story. They then build a strategic plan using the other narrative elements leading to that vision.

Improv topics:
- Accepting offers
- Storytelling
- Trust

Purpose:
- Team building
- Creativity
- Communication
- Needs assessment
- Problem solving

Supplies:
- A flip chart and pens

Time:
- 30–60 minutes

Number of players:
- 2–20

Game flow:
- Agree on a vision (see 'Vision weaving' as a possible activity).
- Display the story spine (see Chapter 6 for more details):
  Once upon a time…
  Every day…
  But one day…
  Because of that… (Repeat as often as desired.)
  Until finally…
  Ever since then…
- Plug the vision into the 'Ever since then' section.
- Tell the participants that 'Once upon a time' is now, and they are going to work on how to get from there to the end of the story, using the rest of the spine as a guide to creating an action plan.

- Have individuals create the story one sentence at a time around the circle. For the 'Because of that' section, you may have each individual suggest how the person to his or her right contributed to achieving the happy ending.

Variations:
- Have individuals share or write their own version of the story, telling how they will personally contribute to the vision.
- Have groups of three to five participants create the vision story separately and then present it to the group.
- Use the spine as a guide on a much larger scale, doing activities for the current state, strategic planning and visioning.

Tips:
- Choose a format that maximizes the individual's involvement.
- Spend time forming and agreeing on a vision before you begin.
- Decide on the level of practicality that you are looking for. Is this an idea-generation session or a realistic problem-solving one?
- Make sure you are capturing all the ideas.

Suggested debrief questions:
- How was this process different from other visioning sessions?
- What felt right?
- What still feels troubling?
- How much of what we created feels possible?
- What do we still need to do?
- Has your picture of the future changed at all?
- How do you feel about your ability personally to affect the realization of the vision?

Source:
- StoryNet LLC, based on Kenn Adams's story spine structure

The story spine story

Overview:
- Participants use this sentence-at-a-time template to create well-structured stories, individually or collaboratively (see Chapter 6 for discussion).

Improv topics:
- Storytelling
- Accepting offers
- Listening and awareness
- Spontaneity

Purpose:
- Warm-up
- Team building
- Creativity
- Communication
- Needs assessment
- Problem solving
- Review
- Closing

Supplies:
- A flip chart, slide or handout with the story spine recorded

Time:
- 10–60 minutes

Number of players:
- 1–5 per group

Game flow:
- Present the story spine:
  Once upon a time…
  Every day…
  But one day…
  Because of that… (Repeat three times, or as often as necessary.)
  Until finally…
  Ever since then…
  And the moral of the story is… (optional).
- Have participants create a story one sentence at a time using the cue words to begin each sentence.

Variations:
- The story spine can be used any time stories are incorporated into a design. For example:
  - As a review activity, divide the participants into groups and have them create a story that illustrates an important learning point.
  - Individually, have participants write the story of the workshop to assess learning, or before the workshop begins as a way of assessing needs.
  - As a trainer, speaker or presenter, use the spine to create anecdotes or to hone existing ones.
  - As a visioning and problem-solving tool, the story spine can offer structure for brainstorming and action planning (see 'Story visioning').

Tips:
- Some people love structure, whereas others feel limited by it. Use the story spine merely as a support tool, allowing participants to deviate from it if they wish.
- If you are concentrating on storytelling, you may wish to analyse the structure (see Chapter 6). Otherwise, the story spine can be presented as a tool without much explanation.

Suggested debrief questions:
- How did the structure help or hinder you?
- Was the process of creating a story easier or harder than you expected?
- What is the value of using stories in learning?
- What value does this structure provide?
- What are the other elements of good storytelling? (Details, emotion, presentation skills.)

Source:
- Originally created by Kenn Adams, and adapted by StoryNet LLC

True or false

Overview:
- Participants take turns telling one true story and one false. The rest of the group guesses which is which.

Improv topics:
- Listening and awareness
- Storytelling
- Non-verbal behaviour

Purposes:
- Team building
- Creativity
- Communication

Supplies:
- None

Time:
- 15 minutes preparation (preparation may be assigned ahead of time) plus 10 minutes per participant

Number of players:
- Variable

Game flow:
- Assign each participant to think of a true story and a false story.
- Have the participants take turns telling both of their stories. The other members of the group guess which they think is the true story and which is the false one.

Variations:
- Have three or four people tell stories, one of which is true. The observers guess which one it is.
- Have each participant think of a story and then come up with a one-sentence title or description (eg 'I once tried to buy a mink coat for $39'). Then, in groups of three or four, have the participants choose one of those titles that they wish to work with. The person who owns that title tells the story, while the others in the group tell made-up stories based on the same title. Observers guess which story is true.

- Play the above with real objects. Each participant brings an object. The group decides on its favourite, and then each person tells the story of why that object is his or hers – the real owner telling a true story and the others making one up.

Tips:
- Encourage participants to create really false stories, rather than just changing minor details of a true one.
- In addition to discussing which stories were believable, you may choose to discuss which were most compelling. They may or may not be the same.
- You may choose to give people time to create stories ahead of time, to plan in class or to improvise on the spot.

Suggested debrief questions:
- How easy was it to deceive people? Why?
- As observers, how did you decide which story was true?
- Did you have more fun telling true or made-up stories?
- What clues other than words were received as to the trustworthiness of the speaker?
- Which stories were most compelling? Were those mostly the true ones or not?
- Which qualities make a story compelling?
- How important is it that a story is true?
- What can you do if you want to make up a story to maintain credibility?

Source:
- General acting training

Vision weaving

Overview:
- In a circle, participants create a sensory montage of their desired state. Individuals randomly shout out attributes of their ideal vision of the future. Examples are: 'Customers tell their friends about our service', 'Our stock has risen 300 per cent', 'We bring our dogs to work' and 'There is fresh bread baking in the kitchen.'

Improv topics:
- Trust
- Spontaneity
- Accepting offers
- Listening and awareness

Purpose:
- Warm-up
- Team building
- Creativity
- Communication
- Needs assessment
- Problem solving
- Closing

Supplies:
- A flip chart and pens or a tape recorder

Time:
- 10–20 minutes

Number of players:
- 2–20

Game flow:
- Seat the participants in a circle.
- Provide a specific focus for the vision (eg 'our office in 2010' or 'our organization one year from now').
- Tell the participants that in a minute you will ask them to close their eyes. You would like them, at their leisure, to offer details about their ideal vision of that environment.
- Tell them that anyone can say anything at any time, with the exception that no one may offer more than two ideas in a row.

- Remind them that they are not committed to any of the ideas stated, so that they should just let the suggestions wash over them without stopping to object or evaluate. There will be time for that later.
- Let them know that you may pepper the activity with questions.
- Begin.
- As the activity slows down naturally, tell the group that it is about to end. Ask if anyone has anything else they would like to add.
- Debrief.

Variations:
- Guide the image generation more specifically by offering scenarios and asking questions continuously. (Example: 'You are in the entrance hall. You overhear two clients talking about your company. What do they say?')
- Have groups of two to five participants vision separately and then come together and share.
- Have individuals write down their individual visions and then swap papers randomly and share.

Tips:
- Coach the group to take its time and allow silence.
- Offer questions that spur the group to think about the following:
  - what they see;
  - what they hear (eg what people at work say or what they themselves say when they go home);
  - what smells are in the air;
  - what they are able to do;
  - how they feel.
- If there are a few members of the group who dominate, you may want to go around the circle in order for a while.
- To capture the vision, write down what is said or invite someone outside the group to do so. You may also choose to tape-record the session for later transcription.
- Visioning sessions only lead to change when they are operationalized. Plan to use the information generated here in strategic planning activities.

Suggested debrief questions:
- How do you feel?
- How was that process?
- What do you think about that picture of the future?

- What elements really sparked your passion?
- What feels possible?
- What surprised you?
- Anything else you want to add?

Source:
- Rebecca Stockley and Michael Vance's 'Five sense visioning' exercise

Warm-up: physical and vocal

Overview:
- This is a general set of exercises for the voice and body to be done in a group setting or individually as ongoing conditioning or preparation for presentations.

Improv topics:
- Non-verbal behaviour
- Spontaneity
- Listening and awareness

Purpose:
- Ice-breaker
- Warm-up
- Energy builder
- Communication

Supplies:
- None

Time:
- 7–10 minutes

Number of players:
- 1–200

Game flow:
- Have the participants stand in a circle in a grounded, neutral position – feet shoulder-width apart, knees bent slightly, shoulders back and down, head loose and balanced, eyes straight ahead.
- Lead them through a series of slow stretches, head and shoulder rolls, etc. For example:
  - Stretch to each side, holding each position for a count of 10.
  - Roll the head gently around, remembering to lift it slightly at the back so that the neck is not crunched.
  - Roll down the spine, so that you are hanging from the waist. Let your head drop. Shake out your shoulders and then slowly roll up, stacking each vertebra one on top of the other, bringing the head up last.
  - Swing your arms back in the same direction for a count of eight, then forward and then one in one direction, one in the other.

-   Shake out each leg and rotate the ankles, swing from the knees and then swing from the hips.
-   Bend the knees and swing the hips back and forth, right and left, in circles.
-   Isolate the rib cage and move it side to side, front and back, round in circles.
-   Shake out the entire body.
- Lead the group through a series of vocal exercises. For example:
  -   During the above physical exercises, encourage the participants to breathe deeply from their diaphragm and to release sounds ('ahhh', 'mmmm') as they exhale.
  -   Massage the face and jaw. Make big faces and scrunched faces.
  -   Hum from the lowest part of the vocal register to the highest.
  -   Blow through your lips.
  -   Practise tongue twisters as clearly as possible.
  -   Breathe in on a count of four, hold for four, breathe out for eight and hold empty for four. Work up to patterns of 8, 8, 16, 8 and then 16, 16, 32, 16.
  -   Have the participants practise speaking to each other from across the room, so that they can be understood without shouting, but with strong, supported voices.

Variations:
- There are a number of vocal training publications that can be consulted for more specific exercises and information.

Tips:
- People can feel vulnerable doing these kinds of drills. Make sure to model the exercises as you go, and acknowledge the risk.
- The more specific you can be as you lead the group, the safer they will feel.
- If anyone feels light-headed, instruct the person to take a break and have a seat.

Suggested debrief questions:
- How do you feel?
- What is the value of doing these kinds of warm-ups?
- What are two exercises that you can realistically see yourself incorporating into your real life?

Source:
- General acting training

Word drill

Overview:
- This is a straightforward word association game. In groups of three to five, participants take turns sitting in the 'hot seat'. The other participants shoot words at the person in the 'hot seat', and that person responds with the first word or phrase that comes to mind.

Improv topics:
- Spontaneity
- Accepting offers
- Trust

Purpose:
- Warm-up
- Energy builder
- Creativity
- Communication

Supplies:
- None

Time:
- 6–12 minutes

Number of players:
- 3–5 per group

Game flow:
- Arrange the participants into groups of three to five.
- Ask one of them to stand facing the others, who form a horseshoe in front of that person.
- One by one the other members of the group throw out a word. The person in the 'hot seat' responds to each word with the first word or phrase that comes to mind.
- After a few minutes, the participants switch and a new person takes the 'hot seat'.

Variations:
- Play in pairs shooting words back and forth.

- Play in a large group, with one person walking down the line of other participants, responding to a word from each one and finally taking his or her place at the end of the line to participate in throwing out words for the next person.

Tips:
- Set up the activity as a content-less one. Assure participants that the words they say will not be analysed.
- Coach participants to respond as quickly as possible.
- Coach participants to respond without saying 'um' or 'ah'.
- Coach the individuals who are giving words to shout them out as quickly as possible and to give unrelated words as much as possible, to keep the 'hot seat' person off balance. Let the group know that their job is to provide that person with a workout, so the group may think of their words ahead of time if they find that helps.
- Watch the participants to see when they have had enough and have them switch to the next person.

Suggested debrief questions:
- How did it feel to be in the 'hot seat'?
- How did if feel to give words?
- How did you censor yourself?
- What happened as the exercise continued?
- How do you feel now?

Source:
- Matt Smith, Seattle improviser

Word patterns

Overview:
- In a circle, the participants create a pattern of passing a word around the circle. Then they create a different pattern with a different word and pass both patterns simultaneously. Then a third pattern is added and so on.

Improv topics:
- Listening and awareness
- Trust
- Accepting offers

Purpose:
- Ice-breaker
- Warm-up
- Energy builder
- Team building
- Communication

Supplies:
- None

Time:
- 15–20 minutes

Number of players:
- 6–20

Game flow:
- Have the participants stand in a circle.
- Point to someone across the circle and say 'you'.
- That person puts a hand on his or her head to indicate that he or she has been pointed to, and then points to someone else across the circle. This process continues till everyone has been incorporated into the pattern. The last person points back to the first person.
- After the pattern has been established, have the participants repeat it a few times without the pointing, so that each person says 'you' to the same person each time, passing the word through the pattern like a ball.
- Next initiate a new pattern by pointing to a new person and saying something that falls into a category (eg animals, colours, conflict resolution techniques). This time each person says a different word, but one that fits into the category.

- That new person puts a hand on his or her head to indicate that he or she has been pointed to, and then points to someone else across the circle. This pattern continues till everyone has been incorporated into it, with each person pointing to a different partner.
- Then both patterns are passed around the circle simultaneously.
- Continue to create and add a third and fourth pattern if the group is willing and able.

Variations:
- Create three patterns and then ask people to walk to their partner's place as they pass the original 'you' pattern. This adds a level of difficulty since the layout of the circle will change.
- Start patterns without identifying a category, and have one emerge from the words that participants associate and add.
- Play with closed eyes.
- Play using the word 'you' in the first pattern, 'me' in the second and 'us' in the third.

Tips:
- Remember to check each pattern alone, before combining patterns.
- Remind participants to point to different people each time.
- Continue to pass the words through the circle more than once a round, to get momentum going when the group is doing well.
- Coach participants to take responsibility for their partners receiving and passing along each word.

Suggested debrief questions:
- What did this feel like?
- What helped us achieve our task?
- What hindered us?
- What obstacles did we encounter?
- How did we help each other?
- How is this like collaborating in real life?

Source:
- Adapted from Theatresports worldwide and Carol Hazenfield

You're out

Overview:
- Groups of participants role-play a meeting in which they compete to belong to and exclude others from the group.

Improv topics:
- Trust
- Non-verbal behaviour
- Listening and awareness
- Storytelling
- Accepting offers

Purpose:
- Team building
- Communication

Supplies:
- None

Time:
- 3–5 minutes per scene

Number of players:
- 3 participants per scene

Game flow:
- Ask for three volunteers.
- Give them a setting for a role-play – a meeting, a holiday party, a school class.
- Instruct each person that the objective is to align him- or herself with someone and exclude the third person.
- Play the scene.
- Debrief.

Variations:
- Play so that one group rejects another group.
- Play so that one person rejects a group of others.
- Play with one person rejecting one other.
- Set specific scenarios, such as a trainer being rejected by workshop participants, a new employee being rejected by a team, a woman being rejected by her male counterparts at a bar.

Tips:
- This is an excellent exercise for exploring group dynamics. It is also very powerful. Be sure to create a safe space and debrief thoroughly. Ask the participants' permission to play, and let them know ahead of time what they will be doing.
- Play for short stretches of time, changing participants often.
- The experience can be a revelation for those watching as well as those playing. Make sure you include the observers in the debrief.

Suggested debrief questions:
- How did it feel to be excluded?
- How did it feel to belong?
- How did it feel to exclude?
- How did it feel to watch the scene?
- What techniques did you find for belonging?
- What behaviours led to exclusion?
- How do these dynamics play out in your workplace?

Source:
- Adapted from Viola Spolin's 'Rejection' game and the work of Keith Johnstone, Diane Rachel and Theatresports

Appendix

Table A.1 Activities: improv topics

Activity	Trust	Spontaneity	Accepting offers	Listening and awareness	Story-telling	Non-verbal behaviour	Page
Accept this!		X	X				154
Ask a silly question	X	X	X				119
Awareness quiz				X			121
Ball ball	X		X	X			123
Ball toss	X		X	X			25
Blindfold walk	X			X		X	125
But vs and			X	X			127
Character creation	X	X	X	X	X	X	129
Circle mirror	X			X		X	132
Classic mirror	X			X		X	134
Colour/advance		X	X	X	X		94
Conducted narrative		X	X	X	X		136
Conversation weave			X	X	X		138
Declare yourself	X			X		X	140
Elimination lists	X	X		X			142
Emotional meeting	X	X	X	X		X	144
Experts	X	X	X	X	X	X	57
Gibberish press conference		X	X		X	X	146
Giving gifts	X	X	X			X	148
Group counting	X			X			77
Hum circle	X	X	X	X			150
I failed!	X	X					40
Idea circle		X					152
Invisible balls	X	X	X	X		X	32
Neutral status scene				X	X	X	154
One-sided scene			X	X		X	156
One-word-at-a-time exercises		X	X	X	X		158
Paired drawing		X	X			X	160
Picture maths		X	X	X	X		162
Picture poetry		X	X	X	X		164

Table A.1 *continued*

Activity	Trust	Spontaneity	Accepting offers	Listening and awareness	Story-telling	Non-verbal behaviour	Page
Safety zone		X	X			X	166
Slap pass	X	X	X	X	X	X	168
Speaking in unison		X	X	X	X		51
Speech tag		X	X	X	X	X	170
Spontaneous marketing		X	X				172
Stats	X	X					22
Status cards				X		X	107
Status demo	X			X		X	174
Status pass	X					X	176
Story exchange	X		X	X	X	X	67
Story of your name	X				X		20
Story seeds			X		X		178
Story visioning	X		X		X		180
The story spine story		X	X	X	X		181
Three-word stories		X	X	X	X		89
True or false				X	X	X	184
Vision weaving	X	X	X	X			186
Warm-up: physical and vocal		X		X		X	189
Word drill	X	X	X				191
Word patterns	X		X	X			193
You're out	X		X	X	X	X	195

Table A.2 Activities: training uses

Activity	Supplies	Time	Number of players	Ice-breaker	Team building	Creativity	Communication	Review	Needs assessment	Problem solving	Energy builder	Warm-up	Closing	Page
Accept this!	None	8–15 mins.	Pairs		X	X	X				X	X	X	154
Ask a silly question	None	3–8 mins.	Various	X	X	X					X	X		119
Awareness quiz	None	3–5 mins.	Pairs		X	X	X				X	X		121
Ball ball	A soft ball	7–15 mins.	4–20	X	X		X	X	X		X	X	X	123
Ball toss	5–10 soft juggling balls or sacks	10–30 mins.	6–20	X	X		X				X	X	X	25
Blindfold walk	None	10–20 mins.	Pairs		X		X					X		125
But vs and	None	4–8 mins.	Various		X	X	X							127
Character creation	None	10–20 mins.	2–20		X	X	X					X		129
Circle mirror	None	5–7 mins.	6–20		X	X	X				X			132
Classic mirror	None	8–15 mins.	Pairs		X	X	X					X		134
Colour/advance	A flip chart, slide or handout	5–15 mins.	Pairs			X	X	X	X	X				94
Conducted narrative	None	3–6 mins. per round	4–5 per round		X	X	X	X				X		136
Conversation weave	None	8–15 mins. per group	3–4 per group		X	X	X							138
Declare yourself	None	5–15 mins.	3–20	X	X	X	X	X	X			X	X	140
Elimination lists	None	6–12 mins.	4–20, plus observers	X	X	X	X	X			X	X		142
Emotional meeting	Chairs and table, flip chart (all optional)	5–10 mins. per group	3–5 per group		X		X				X			144

Table A.2 *continued*

Activity	Supplies	Time	Number of players	Ice-breaker	Team building	Creativity	Communication	Review	Needs assessment	Problem solving	Energy builder	Warm-up	Closing	Page
Experts	Two chairs	7–15 mins. per group	Pairs		X	X	X	X	X	X				57
Gibberish press conference	None	5–30 mins.	Pairs		X	X	X	X			X			146
Giving gifts	None	5–15 mins.	Pairs	X	X	X	X					X		148
Group counting	None	3–10 mins.	4–20		X		X						X	77
Hum circle	None	5–10 mins.	4–16		X		X					X	X	150
I failed!	None	2–5 mins.	2–200	X	X	X	X			X	X	X		40
Idea circle	One object	20–30 secs. per participant per round	10–20		X	X		X			X	X		152
Invisible balls	None	5–20 mins.	4–20	X	X	X	X				X	X		32
Neutral status scene	Handouts, flip chart or slide	15–30 mins.	Pairs		X		X							154
One-sided scene	None	3–5 mins. per role-play	Pairs		X		X							156
One-word-at-a-time exercises	None	5–30 mins.	2–20		X	X	X	X			X	X		158
Paired drawing	Coloured pens and paper, flip chart	10–30 mins.	Pairs		X	X	X							160
Picture maths	None	10–15 mins.	Trios			X					X	X		162
Picture poetry	None	4–10 mins.	Pairs		X	X	X					X		164
Safety zone	None	3–6 mins.	8–100		X						X	X		166
Slap pass	None	5–15 mins.	5–25		X	X	X				X	X		168

Table A.2 *continued*

Activity	Supplies	Time	Number of players	Ice-breaker	Team building	Creativity	Commun-ication	Review	Needs assess-ment	Problem solving	Energy builder	Warm-up	Closing	Page
Speaking in unison	None	3–5 mins. per group	3–5 per group		X	X	X	X			X	X		51
Speech tag	None	3–5 mins. per group	3–5 per group		X	X	X	X						170
Spontaneous marketing	Flip charts (one per group), markers	15–20 mins. plus 3 mins. per group to share	2–5 per group	X	X	X	X							172
Stats	One chair per participant	15–30 mins.	6–20	X	X		X		X		X	X		22
Status cards	1 playing card per person	10–20 mins.	5–100		X		X				X	X		107
Status demo	None	5–15 mins.	5–100		X	X	X					X		174
Status pass	None	5–15 mins.	2–20		X	X	X					X		176
Story exchange	3×5 cards, pens	25–50 mins.	10–20	X	X	X	X							67
Story of your name	None	1–2 mins. per participant	Variable	X	X		X					X		20
Story seeds	Pens and paper	10–20 mins.	Variable			X	X	X	X	X				178
Story visioning	A flip chart and pens	30–60 mins.	2–20		X	X	X	X	X	X				180
The story spine story	A flip chart, slide or handout with the story spine recorded	10–60 mins.	1–5 per group		X	X	X	X	X	X		X	X	181
Three-word stories	None	5–7 mins.	Pairs		X	X	X	X						89

Table A.2 *continued*

Activity	Supplies	Time	Number of players	Ice-breaker	Team building	Creativity	Communication	Review	Needs assessment	Problem solving	Energy builder	Warm-up	Closing	Page
True or false	None	15 mins. preparation (or preparation assigned ahead of time) plus 10 mins. per participant	Variable		X	X	X							184
Vision weaving	A flip chart and pens or a tape recorder	10–20 mins.	2–20		X	X	X		X	X		X	X	186
Warm-up: physical and vocal	None	7–10 mins.	1–200	X			X				X	X		189
Word drill	None	6–12 mins.	3–5 per group			X	X				X	X		191
Word patterns	None	15–20 mins.	6–20	X	X		X				X	X		193
You're out	None	3–5 mins. per scene	3 per scene		X		X							195

References

Allred, K (1996, unpublished) Class notes: negotiation, Columbia University

Armstrong, A (1992) *Managing by Storying Around: A new method of leadership*, Doubleday, New York

Blatner, A and Blatner, A (1997) *The Art of Play: Helping adults reclaim imagination and spontaneity* (rev edn), Brunner/Mazel, New York

Cameron, J (1992) *The Artist's Way: A spiritual path to higher creativity*, Jeremy P Tarcher/Putnam, New York

Campbell, J (1973) *A Hero with a Thousand Faces*, Bollingen Series/Princeton University Press, Princeton, NJ

Deci, E L and Flaste, R (1996) *Why We Do What We Do: Understanding self-motivation*, Penguin, New York

French, J R P and Raven, B H (1959) The basis of social power, in *Studies in Social Power*, ed D Cartwright, Institute for Social Research, Ann Arbor, MI

Hall, D (1996) *Jump Start Your Brain*, Warner Books, New York

Halpern, C, Close, D and Johnson, K (1994) *Truth in Comedy: The manual of improvisation*, Meriwether Publishing, Colorado Springs, CO

Johnstone, K (1979) *Impro: Improvisation and the theatre*, Theatre Arts Books, New York

Lamott, A (1994) *Bird by Bird*, Anchor Books, New York

Mehrabian, A (1971) *Silent Messages*, Wadsworth, Belmont, CA

Nierenberg, G I and Calero, H *How to Read a Person Like a Book*, Pocket Books

Parkin, M (1998) *Tales for Trainers: Using stories and metaphors to facilitate learning*, Kogan Page, London

Schank, R C (1990) *Tell Me a Story*, Northwestern University Press, Evanston, IL

Seligman, M E P (1998) *Learned Optimism: How to change your mind and your life*, Pocket Books, New York

Spolin, V (1983) *Improvisation for the Theater*, Northwestern University Press, Evanston, IL

Stockley, R (1989) *Improvisation through TheatreSports*, Thespis Productions, Puyallup, WA

Suzuki, S (1985) *Zen Mind, Beginner's Mind: Informal talks on Zen meditation and practice*, Weatherhill, New York

Vogler, C (1998) *The Writer's Journey: Mythic structure for writers*, Michael Wiese Productions, Studio City, CA

Westen, D (1996) *Psychology: Mind, brain and culture*, 2nd edn, John Wiley & Sons, New York

Wiesel, E (1966) *The Gates of the Forest*, tr F Frenaye, Schocken Books, New York

Further reading

Badaracco, J L (1997) *Defining Moments: When managers must choose between right and right*, Harvard Business School Press, Boston, MA

Bal, M (1985) *Narratology: Introduction to the theory of narrative*, University of Toronto Press, Buffalo, NY

Bruner, J (1990) *Acts of Meaning*, Harvard University Press, Cambridge, MA

Burns, J M (1978) *Leadership*, Harper Torchbooks, New York

Johnstone, K (1999) *Impro for Storytellers*, Theatre Arts Books, New York

Mellon, N (1992) *The Art of Storytelling*, Element, Boston, MA

Sen, A (1999) *Development as Freedom*, Alfred A Knopf, New York

Vroom, V H and Deci, E L, eds (1992) *Management and Motivation*, Penguin Books, New York

Index